FAITH + HUSTLE

A 21-Day Devotional for the Fun, Fly, Fabulous Female Entrepreneur

BY ARIAN SIMONE

For all the fearless, fun, fly, fabulous female entrepreneurs!

Acknowledgements

I give honor to God for giving me the vision and direction to author this book. I am thankful to all my family and friends for their everlasting support in all that I do. For every spiritual mentor who taught me the importance of applying my faith as an ingredient for success, I thank you. To all the fearless female entrepreneurs who shared their story as inspiration to the readers, I am forever grateful.

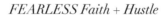

Hustle as it pertains to this book means to work energetically.

We already know that faith without works is dead so Faith + Hustle (Energetic Works) is ALIVE

INTRODUCTION

I am Arian Simone and This Is My Fearless Journey.

And they overcame him by the blood of the Lamb, and by the word of their testimony…

REVELATION 12:11 (KJV)

I feel that it's important to share my testimony and I encourage others to do so as well because it might just be what someone needs to hear to elevate their life.

I was born and raised in Detroit, Michigan with the spirit of entrepreneurship. I have been selling things since I was a child. I sold poinsettias to parents in middle school. I was a top sales representative for Express in high school. I sold Mary Kay Cosmetics my senior year of high school and, while in college, I opened a retail apparel boutique in the mall.

After college, I moved to Los Angeles in January 2004 with a marketing job working for Nelly's Apple Bottoms Jeans. After one month of employment, the company was sold; I was laid off and I had no money. By April 2004, I moved to my car from the apartment I could no longer afford. I sold my clothes and belongings so I could eat and put gas in my car. Never would I have imagined that all this would happen to me. There I was, fully educated having attended undergraduate and graduate school and I had no job. I applied for over 150 jobs and no one hired me. I tried temp agencies. I was on welfare and food stamps. My car broke down. I checked into a shelter. I called my mother one day and told her that I didn't even see the purpose of living if this is what life was like.

Through this experience, my relationship with Christ grew very strong. I was without a place to live for seven months. Around late July, early August, someone who knew of me from Apple Bottoms Jeans referred me to their spouse for some public relations and marketing work. They sent other referrals and within two weeks I had about five to seven projects going on. I immediately got the car out of the shop and then moved into an office space with the help of my sorority sister ND Brown.

That October, I lived out of the office. By the end of November, I was able to afford an apartment. The office was a blessing. It was in a high rise in central L.A. and housed the most happening hip-hop station in L.A., 100.3 The Beat, on its 19th floor.

I woke up every morning and networked with whatever celebrities were at the radio station for the Steve Harvey Morning Show. I made plenty of contacts.

Then one day Coach Carter (the real Coach Ken Carter on which the movie Coach Carter was based) was on my floor and he shared with me how movie studios outsource people for public relations. He had me help out with some projects for the movie prior to its release. From this exposure, I then contacted Florida A & M University alumni Will Packer and Rob Hardy who I knew were in the movie business and informed them of the work I'd been doing.

From there my company was blessed to work on Stomp the Yard and This Christmas. Sony Pictures became a client and we have done PR and marketing campaigns for Takers, Quantum of Solace 007, Hancock, Seven Pounds, First Sunday, Taking of Pelham 123 and the list goes on. We have provided services to plenty of celebrities from Lil Wayne to Chris Brown and have put on some very grand, star-studded events surrounding the Oscars and Grammy Awards.

All of these experiences have led me to know that being FEARLESS has been a key ingredient to my success, and I have made it my mission to encourage all to embrace a FEARLESS lifestyle, because to whom much is given, much is required.

For God has not given us the spirit of fear but of power and of love and of sound mind.

2 TIMOTHY 1:7 (NKJV)

MY WHY FOR THIS BOOK

People always ask me about my morning routine. I find that question very interesting because it comes up so often and well, here is the answer.
The first part of my day is spent with God. I start my day anchored and centered. I read the Our Daily Bread. I read it online now but started off with the little book. I got this from my grandmother as I saw her read it all the time. Next, I pray. I have scriptures posted in my prayer closet that I recite. Then I go into prayer. I have very transparent conversations with God; God is my homie. The Bible tells us to worship in spirit and truth and I give God my honest truth. Why not? He knows it anyway.

Depending on the day, I also meditate, and I exercise three to five days out of the week. I do cardio in a gym or outside. I don't start my day on emails or social media. When I do that, I end up spending the entire day responding to the day versus being in control of my day. I could easily go all day and not get my to-do list done which can cause a snowball effect. Instead, I prepare a to-do list the day before. My list is arranged according to time of day. As a female entrepreneur, it's imperative I am productive and get things crossed off my list. I do not get notifications on my phone for social media as I don't want to be prompted to react.

In 2009 I stopped doing music publicity, and I stopped my email from going to my phone. I now only read emails on the computer so that I can be in complete control of when I choose to respond and not react.

I can remember being on tour with Chris Brown back in 2006 and every morning faithfully I had a sermon playing. My best friend Karia visited me while on tour and came to my room and saw I had a sermon playing. She was so happy to see in the midst of all that was going on around me that I remained grounded. I laughed because honestly I didn't even view it that way; I was just being me.

Though I go to church regularly, I understand I am no one's typical church girl, and this definitely is not your grandmother's devotional. But God calls many of us to be His light from all backgrounds.

So, long story short, this book is me sharing with you a piece of my morning routine in hopes to add more value to your life.

Enjoy the 21-Day Journey!

Love Always,
Arian Simone

Prayer for Dreamers and Visionaries

My prayer today is for every dreamer and visionary. I pray that you see the provision that God has put in place for the vision that He has given you. I pray that you know that you are operating from a place of abundance and never a place of lack. I pray that you do what you can with what you have because God supplies all your needs according to His riches in glory through Christ Jesus. I declare and decree that you are walking in the anointing and the gifts that you have been given by the Almighty. I declare and decree that your gifts are making room for you and bring you before great men. I declare and decree that you will shine and not dim your light for anyone, for you are needed in this world. I pray that you know creation is waiting for you to take your place so the people you are called to serve can receive what they are waiting on in Jesus' name. Amen.

Day 1
Seize the Moment

You have to seize the moment. Many opportunities can come your way, but a moment can never be relived.

SCRIPTURE

Jesus said, "No procrastination. No backward looks. You can't put God's kingdom off till tomorrow. Seize the day."

LUKE 9:62 (MSG)

Seizing the moment is so important to me because I always say that many opportunities may come but a moment cannot be relived. I will never forget when I lived in Los Angeles. I lived in an office at 5900 Wilshire on the 26th floor. On the 19th floor of the building was this happening hip-hop station, 100.3FM The Beat. Every celebrity you could imagine came in and out of the building. And, because I was starting a PR and marketing business with a focus in the entertainment industry, this opportunity to be near this particular radio station was perfect for me. I seized the moment every chance I got to interact with them.

Every single morning, security would let me know which celebrities were in the building. They would call up to the office, and say, "Hey, Arian, Kanye West is in the building" or "Hey, Arian, Nick Cannon is in the building." I'd run downstairs, shower at LA Fitness on the bottom floor, and get ready to head on to the radio station. I made it happen.

You need to be ready when opportunity knocks. You have heard it before and I'll say it again, you need to stay ready so you don't have to get ready. You can't just be in the right place at the right time. You need to be the right person, in the right place, at the right time. Ask yourself if you prepared for everything you prayed for. When opportunity knocks, you want to be ready. When you see the door open, don't just walk through it. You need to run through it because you need to seize the moment!

The word seize is a verb which means "to take hold of suddenly." The phrase "seize the moment" is telling you to take hold of that exact moment quickly. As I said in the beginning, many opportunities can come but a moment cannot be relived. The reality is we can't rewind the hands of time. If a business opportunity exists that you know you are prepared for and would be a game changer for your business, release any fear and move forward with confidence. Move on your intuition; seize your moment.

Had I ignored the opportunities when I was living in the office, I would have lost out on them. The security officers who called to let me know which celebrities were in the building eventually would have stopped calling me. Had I told them not this week or to call back next week, they would have stopped giving me tips on who was coming in the building. The lesson here is to rise to the occasion.

The Bible gives many examples of how to seize moments when certain opportunities come your way. The first command that God gives us in the Bible is to be fruitful and multiply. Those moments of increase that require your application to appear in the form of opportunities.

BIBLICAL EXAMPLE OF SEIZING BUSINESS OPPORTUNITIES

In Matthew 25:14-30 there is a famous passage on the parable of talents. For those who may not know the story, there is a master who called his servants. To one servant, he gave five talents (talent is unit of currency). He gave two talents to another, and he gave one talent to yet another. The servant who received five talents went at once and traded with them and made an additional five talents. The servant with two talents doubled his also. But the servant with one talent buried his talent and did not produce more.

When opportunities come your way, your goal is to leverage and maximize them. In the biblical passage, the direction to increase what the servants were given was not stated at all. No one told the servant with five talents to go and make more. No one told the servant with two talents to go and make more. They were able to recognize an opportunity and make the best of it. Because they acted without any direction at all, you could assume that they were previously programmed to do so. Humans are creatures of habit. We as business owners have to get in the habit of seizing and maximizing whenever opportunities are presented.The servant that buried his one talent was reprimanded for not seeing the opportunity and doing more with it. Again remember, no one told the servants to increase what they had. It was an unstated expectation of the master. The master expected them to all see the opportunity of increase. For the servants who came back with double, he rewarded them greatly and entrusted them with more. The master said because they had been faithful over few they were being made ruler over many. Talking about being fruitful and multiplying!

Now, don't get me wrong. We are all human; we make mistakes. At some point, everyone is bound to miss an opportunity or another. Please don't beat yourself up. It happens but it doesn't have to be a habit. Dust yourself off and move forward with a keen eye at recognizing opportunities and seizing the moment.

The more God sees you maximizing opportunities, the more opportunities He can trust you with. He will send more because you have displayed that you can be trusted.

PRAYER

Dear Lord, I pray that you open my eyes to see every opportunity you place in front of me. Lord, fully prepared me for all the blessings you have in store for me. I choose to walk boldly and with confidence for Lord I know that my confidence shall be richly rewarded as I seize the moment. In Jesus' name I pray, amen.

DECLARATIONS

To be recited out loud in front of the mirror with your right hand on your heart.

I SEIZE THE MOMENT.

I AM AN ACTION TAKER.

I AM PREPARED.

I AM CONFIDENT.

I SEE OPPORTUNITIES AND MOVE ON THEM.

EXERCISES

List 3 Opportunities You See That Can Be Leveraged

List 3 Action Steps You Can Take to Prepare

FEARLESS FEMALE ENTREPRENEUR SPOTLIGHT

Claire Sulmers

Author, Lifestyle Curator & Entrepreneur

I remember the day like it was yesterday. It was a cold, dreary night in the fall of 2007, and I was sitting in my studio apartment in Paris trying to keep warm. Mini cars zoomed by puddles in the streets, and a couple laughed as they passed by my shuttered windows. Their cheery laughter seemed to mock my dire situation. I sat staring at my laptop, seeing nothing but negative signs and red alert symbols. My bank account was overdrafted, credit cards past due, and I had no money. My site, Fashion Bomb Daily, wasn't at the point yet where it was making any revenue. I had placed advertisement requests on my sidebar, but not one person had taken the bait. I responded to an email from an interested advertiser who was supposed to send over a couple hundred dollars, but after I followed up, there was nothing. I had nothing.

As I stared at my computer screen with the words past due assaulting my corneas, tears rolled down my cheeks. I put my head down as the sobs quickened, and then my anxiety induced episode accelerated. My body lurched as the tears came on uncontrollably. I had graduated from Harvard University, I had worked for 4 years at a well-respected magazine before

I decided to quit my job and chase my dreams of working in fashion to Paris. I sent out my resume every day, but Paris wasn't panning out quite how I had planned. I wasn't just broke, I was in debt, buried deep in a financial, mental, and emotional dark hole with no foreseeable way of getting out.

My sobs and convulsing led me to the ground, where I got on my knees and clasped my hands towards the sky. I cried, "Please GOD. Please GOD. I don't have anything. I pray that you bless me. I pray for prosperity. I pray for unebbing abundance. Please GOD." I desperately begged as I continued to cry, with tears, and now snot running down my puffy face.

"Please GOD," I whimpered, lowering myself closer to the ground until I crumpled into a pile on the floor and fell asleep.

Things hadn't been easy during my whole time in Paris, but this was a new low. My freelance checks weren't coming in, advertisers who said they would pay suddenly disappeared. And bills didn't stop. I had nothing and didn't know when I would have any thing. Sweet sleep seemed to be the only thing that quieted my fears, albeit temporarily.

I woke up the next morning, and felt an empty gnawing in my stomach. I was hungry. I felt around in my pockets and found a few Euro coins, totaling about 5 Euros. I planned out my day, and thought, "I'll send out a few emails this morning, then head out. There is a crepe stand by the Sorbonne that makes ham and cheese crepes with an egg on top for 3 Euro. I can get that, plus a soda, and I should be full." I planned to head out midday, but just as I was committing my plan to memory, my phone rang. It was my friend, Toushi, one of the few friends I had in Paris.

"Hi Claire, how are you?"

"Good, you?"

"Amazing. Was wondering if you wanted to come to church with me?"

I didn't have anything on my schedule and had never been to church before in Paris, so I was game.

"Sure!" I exclaimed. I threw on smart black pants, a white top, and a wool coat, and, after Toushi gave me directions, I met her there. The room was full to the brim with faithful souls from all walks of life. The service began with singing and ended with prayers in French. Afterwards, all the members milled around, greeting each other by a coffee machine and a cookie platter.

"That was great!" I exclaimed to Toushi.

"Wasn't it? I love coming here. I'm glad you enjoyed it," Toushi smiled. Then she paused, "Do you want to come back to my house and eat? My roommate and I are cooking dinner."

I felt my stomach under my threadbare clothes and replied, "YES!"

We left the church's warm meeting room and headed into the Parisian air. In one quick train ride, we were at Toushi's cozy apartment, where her roommate already had rice cooking on the stove and something delicious baking in the oven.

Toushi motioned me to the couch, where I got comfortable. Within minutes, her roommate Ayo came out with a large plate, with every inch covered with chicken, rice and peas, and vegetables. Ayo placed a large glass of juice on the table before me, and handed me a napkin with utensils. I wasted no time filling my stomach until I had to loosen my pants. Just when I almost couldn't eat anymore, Toushi appeared with vanilla ice cream and cookies for dessert. She wrapped up a plate for me to take home.

When I thought I had nothing and that GOD had forgotten me, when I thought I was down to my last few pennies, my friends showed me the true meaning of GOD's love and grace, filling my plate and my cup until it runneth over.

Within a few months after that, I managed to secure an internship at Paris Vogue. Less than a year later, I had found a way to make my blog profitable. By the time I left Paris, I was making enough to live from my blog full time and work for myself. I ultimately enjoyed more prosperity than I ever had before. On my last day in Paris, I got the tattoos "Hope" and "Faith" on my wrists so that I would never forget how GOD showered grace and love on me at a time when I couldn't see any sliver of hope in a sea of dark clouds.

Now, as I experience business setbacks and career tribulations, I remember those times anew. But instead of despair, I now see them as just a part of life. There are no highs without lows, no mountains without valleys. And many times, 'rock bottom' is just preparing your foundation to break you down, strengthen your faith, and then launch your life in a direction beyond your wildest imagination.

Day 2
Visualization

What you visualize, you materialize.

SCRIPTURE

Where there is no vision, the people perish…

PROVERBS 29:18 (KJV)

What you visualize, you materialize. Whether you have a physical vision board or a digital one, or perhaps even a written list of goals and prayers, visualization is definitely a practice you need to implement in your life. This can help you achieve the things you desire to achieve. As mentioned in my book, My Fabulous and Fearless Journey, I was down and out, living out of my car. I often drove around Beverly Hills. Why? Because I believed if someone could live like that, then I could too.

Although I was living out of my car, I always kept grand and beautiful visuals in front of me. I told myself, "I deserve to live like that." I just had to keep it in front of me because what I visualize, I materialize. I had a vision board in 2008 that began to scare me because it started to manifest sooner than I expected. I put people with whom I wanted to work as clientele on this vision board and those people began to seek out my services. I had Jamie Foxx on the board, and would you believe that I got a call asking me to plan a party at his home of course I said yes. Rapper T.I. was also on the board and next thing I know, I got a call to work on the movie Takers, and as you might recall, T.I. was in that movie. Nearly everyone that I'd placed on the board manifested in my life. I still create vision boards to this day.

I must add a very important principle. I also spoke what was on the board and declared those things to be. Also, you must be mindful of what you digest on social media. What is in your social media feeds, your Facebook feeds, your Instagram feeds? You may be digesting some things you do not want to materialize in your life which means you may need to unfollow some people. Just be very mindful, because again: what you visualize, you materialize.

BIBLICAL EXAMPLES

And the LORD answered me, and said, Write the vision, and make it plain upon tables, that he may run that readeth it. For the vision is yet for an appointed time, but at the end it shall speak, and not lie: though it tarry, wait for it; because it will surely come, it will not tarry.

HABAKKUK 2:2-3 KJV

Something magical happens when visions are placed in front of you. When they move from your head to something you can tangibly see, it becomes plain as day. It doesn't have to be a vision board. It can be a business plan, or on an index card, or written on a napkin. It's just important to get it out of your head by placing it on a tangible reminder.

Now to Him who is able to do immeasurably more than all we ask or imagine, according to His power that is at work within us.

EPHESIANS 3:20 (NIV)

There is power in your imagination. You have heard the famous quote: "What the mind can conceive it can achieve." The above Bible verse discusses how God can give you greater things beyond your imagination. If God can do and will do above what you imagine, it is time to raise your level of imagination.

PRAYER

Dear God, I desire to seek all of you. As I seek your face, I seek your eyes. I desire to see the vision that you have for my life. I surrender all, and I choose your will over my will. Manifest the vision in heaven to be here on earth. Thy will be done on earth as it is in heaven. In Jesus' name, amen.

DECLARATIONS

To be recited out loud in front of the mirror with your right hand on your heart.

I CHOOSE GOD'S VISION FOR MY LIFE.

I SEE BEAUTY IN ALL THINGS.

I SEE GREATNESS ALL AROUND ME.

I SEE BLESSINGS IN ABUNDANCE.

I PLACE INSPIRATIONAL VISUALS IN FRONT OF ME.

EXERCISES

1. Let's put work with our faith! Today choose five inspirational visuals to print out and place in front of you. Take out 20 minutes today to meditate on them to be fully manifested in your life and use your voice to declare them in your life now.

2. On an index card, write down your goals. Every morning and night, visualize yourself with them accomplished.

FEARLESS FEMALE ENTREPRENEUR SPOTLIGHT

Promise Tangeman

Graphic & Web Designer, Owner of Go Live HQ,
Co-Founder of Designer Vaca

Standing on the ocean bank on the last day of our trip, I threw a rock into the water symbolizing everything I didn't want to take home with me: fear, worry, and doubt.

I was surprised that these three cliché buzz words were the obstacles that surfaced, considering they had been my eye-rolling trigger points when other women expressed what they were "struggling" with. My inner response in these conversations was often something along the lines of: "OMG! Stop talking in circles and being such a baby about it! Just go do it!" But in this season, I felt differently. I guess you can say I briefly understood the paralyzing anxiety caused by fear, worry and doubt. And for me, they all stemmed from the mother of all cliché buzz words: Leadership. Okay, I'll back the train up a bit and explain. Within the last year, I've had to decide where my business was actually going. For years, I have been a freelance graphic designer, dabbling in different formats of doing business. I've built a business on creating custom designed logos, brands, and websites for small creative businesses. I also developed website themes that are sold in my own online shop SiteHouse. In tandem with SiteHouse, I created a workshop called GO LIVE where people come from all over the country and I help them build, design, and launch their websites in two days. To say I'm thankful would be an understatement.

All of those formats of doing what I love coupled with generating an income are fun, invigorating and challenging. You see, what really gets me up in the morning, is creating. I love the idea of creating something from nothing and pulling ideas from all kinds of places and paving the way for something NEW. The idea of "will this work?" is a captivating concept to me because I love pioneering undiscovered spaces and places. For years, I've been able to explore this question in my day-to-day process of creating an artistic expression. Things like a painting, creating a graphic, or building a website design from the ground up have been my safe go-to places to create. As my career has continued to evolve, I've also found a strong love for the business components of my work. I'd even go as far as to say that I see the business aspect as a new and different form of art and creativity. And that is invigorating.

Like so many small business owners, I've faced the daunting reality that my current infrastructure is challenged to support the possibilities of future growth. Some days it feels like a beautiful disaster. I find myself frequently asking, "Where does it go from here?!?!"

With a lot of trial and error, failure and success, I have to admit that I have struggled to know if I have what it takes to be a "leader" and grow my business into the company that I imagine. Sure, I'm creative, I could have some influence and I could make stuff happen, but, am I meant to be a leader? [Gulp] Cue fear, worry, and doubt. It's possible that I'm being completely melodramatic and that God's vision for this business is to, simply, be a secondary stream of income for me and my family. I could stay lean and mean, giving myself the opportunity to work from home when we start a family. And if that's what God's desire is for me, then I trust Him completely in that gift. But I can't help but think there's more to the story than just coasting.

I have come to the conclusion that I'm not a "leader" in my conventional understanding of the concept. I don't geek out on HR protocols and strategies or respond within the first 20 seconds of an email hitting my inbox. I rarely wake up at 5am to go for a run, do my morning devo, and analyze my databases while delegating all my to-dos all before breakfast. And I definitely haven't written a lengthy book entitled The 5 Best Pathways to a Great Leader.

That's not me. Cue worry, fear, and doubt again. I have built this idea in my mind of what a leader is and what a leader isn't based on things I've read, seen, and experienced in others. I've easily categorized myself in the genre of what a leader isn't and convinced myself of the reasons why I can't grow my small business into a thriving company. Namely because I'm an unconventional leader. I'm a simple art girl, with a few big dreams, who loves to create stuff that helps other people do what they love to do in their lives/ministry/ work. This season has taught me that I have placed too much emphasis on the idea of the word "leadership" instead of just accepting the position and the opportunity that God has naturally wired me to do and put right in front of me.

Maybe the concept of leadership isn't something we should get over-fixated on. Rather, as we courageously step into our unique calling, we'll realize the leadership capacity we need will follow the calling we've been given. So, go grab any and every rock that identifies the places in your life/business/ministry that are holding you back from really launching into all which God wants to do in and through you. Find some deep water and throw those suckers. Personally, I don't have it all figured out. But one thing I know is that I don't want to let fear, worry and doubt be my anchor anymore and you shouldn't either. Stop being a baby about it and just go do it!!!

Day 3
Our Source

God said, "I was just waiting for you to ask me."

SCRIPTURE

Therefore I tell you, do not worry about your life, what you will eat or drink; or about your body, what you will wear. Is not life more than food, and the body more than clothes?

MATTHEW 6:25 (NIV)

God is definitely our source. When I was homeless in 2004 and living out of my car, I called everybody I could think of to help me get out of the situation. But everyone I called was only able to send me $50 or $100 dollars here and there. Now don't get me wrong; I know small amounts over time can add up, and I was very grateful for every single penny in that moment. However, none of that was ever enough to sustain me. I was able to eat, put gas in my car, but I wasn't able to afford a place to live. I had to get still and have a come-to-Jesus meeting because I had nothing else to turn to.

One day I just said, "Okay God, you're going to have to do something major right now in my life." And after enough praying and fasting, I had a breakthrough. God said, "I was just waiting for you to ask me. You keep asking people but if you just ask me, I will send the people," and He did. The next thing you know, I got a call to do PR and marketing, which was pretty much a call of a lifetime. I ended up working for the people who called and they referred me to other people, who referred me to more people, and before I knew it, I was working on five to seven projects within two weeks. I didn't even really know these people. They would have never been on my list of people I was reaching out to. These were not the people that I was calling when I was down and out. I just literally prayed and God moved on my behalf. This is just a friendly reminder that when we get stuck in ruts, we always try to work everything out by ourselves. We have to be reminded sometimes that God is still and always will be our source.

MATTHEW 6:25-34 (NIV)

Therefore I tell you, do not worry about your life, what you will eat or drink; or about your body, what you will wear. Is not life more than food, and the body more than clothes?

Look at the birds of the air; they do not sow or reap or store away in barns, and yet your heavenly Father feeds them. Are you not much more valuable than they?

Can any one of you by worrying add a single hour to your life?

And why do you worry about clothes? See how the flowers of the field grow. They do not labor or spin.

Yet I tell you that not even Solomon in all his splendor was dressed like one of these.

If that is how God clothes the grass of the field, which is here today and tomorrow is thrown into the fire, will he not much more clothe you—you of little faith?

So do not worry, saying, 'What shall we eat?' or 'What shall we drink?' or 'What shall we wear?'

For the pagans run after all these things, and your heavenly Father knows that you need them.

But seek first his kingdom and his righteousness, and all these things will be given to you as well.

Therefore do not worry about tomorrow, for tomorrow will worry about itself. Each day has enough trouble of its own.

PRAYER

Dear God, I want to thank you for always being my source. Thank you for providing the provision for the vision that you have in my life. Thank you for not just providing fish, I also thank you for teaching me to how to fish. Thank you for being the eternal source of all that I need. I am grateful that every good and perfect thing comes from you. Thank you for all these things, in Jesus' name, Amen.

DECLARATIONS

To be recited out loud in front of the mirror with your right hand on your heart.

I AM A CHILD OF GOD.

I AM AWARE THAT GOD IS MY SOURCE.

I AM A RECIPIENT OF GOD'S BLESSINGS.

I AM A RECIPIENT OF GOD'S GRACE

I AM FOCUSED ON ABUNDANCE.

EXERCISE

Journal a situation where God showed Himself faithful in your life. What are you currently asking man for that you should be asking God? Who can you testify to that God is the ultimate source?

FEARLESS FEMALE ENTREPRENEUR SPOTLIGHT

Catarah Coleman & Shoneji Robison

TOLD FROM CATARAH COLEMAN

Co-Owners of Southern Girl Desserts

What I love about God is that His plans aren't ours and it is best just to stop fighting and trust Him! Back in 2007, I was a year into my new PR job and had no desire to be an entrepreneur, none at all. I wanted a steady check, benefits, and my weekends!! But I'd come to discover that my plans and God's plans were headed down two different paths. In early 2007, I became addicted to a show on MSNBC called The Big Idea with Donny Deutsch. I would watch it faithfully and became inspired by the average people who started their businesses with simple ideas and after a few months the seed was planted. My dear friend Arian Simone would always ask me to make her a personal pan of banana pudding and always said, "You should sell these", I would ignore her, but in secret I was racking my brain to figure out what type of business I could start. After months of research this was going to be her answer to generational wealth. God said, "Start a Bakery, you're taking too long". Clearly all the signs pointed toward this, but I didn't see it clearly until June 2007. As I sat in my small Inglewood apartment it became clear that this was going to be my answer to generational wealth.

Entrepreneurship wasn't obsolete from my upbringing. My paternal grandfather owned a multi-million dollar cleaning business and my dad owned a bagel shop for a few years. I just figured that gene never made it to me.

Now that the seed was planted and I accepted the journey, I got busy. I realized God was in on it the entire time, waiting for me to catch up. The very job I started a year earlier funded my new website, business cards, DBA, business license and everything I needed to get started. I then emailed every person in my address book (no Facebook or Instagram) at the time to let them know about my new venture.

Not too long after things started God sent my business partner Shoneji Robison. "I'm so thankful for a partner who serves the same God and has the same vision. What I didn't know was that Shoneji, an acclaimed actress, was in the process of starting a bakery as well and when a mutual friend suggestedwe partner, we met for 30 minutes and the deal was sealed. In the last eleven years Shoneji and I have endured many storms. One of the biggest tests came after we started selling our desserts in a small coffee shop in 2010. In less than six months we shot a show on HGTV, Food Network and sold over 1500 Groupons and of course the devil didn't like that! So in December 2010 after leaving for Christmas vacation, they got a call that they had to cease and desist all sales out of the location. The owners locked the doors and kicked them out. It was later revealed that they weren't happy about HGTV making Shoneji and I the focal point of the show and putting our business name in front of their name on the signage. While all this is happening we have angry Groupon customers, horrible YELP reviews as a result and our episodes on HGTV and Food Network Cupcake Wars were
airing.

What the devil didn't know was that God's angels were watching and right in front of the enemy he prepared a table. In 2012, less than two years after a nasty court battle and finding our way back, we opened a beautiful bakery in the Baldwin Hills Crenshaw Mall.

If we only looked like what we'd been through. Over the years the challenges of business have been difficult and at times we've wanted to give up. Imagine it being my wedding weekend and I find out the account has been sucked dry from daily loan withdraws and I can't meet our $8,000 payroll, but I'm supposed to be happy and enjoying myself.

But inside and out I'm crying, depressed and just sick! I worked nonstop for months without the ability to pay myself. Yes, it happened!

To God be the glory, He has kept His promises and the prayer we've prayed for years is "Lord we trust you and we trust your word." God said His word would not return void. Ya'll God is faithful and he'll never leave nor forsake you. It's now been 11 years in business and we're embarking on our largest grossing year yet, our 6th year in our brick and mortar, our own baking series on Cook-ing Panda, host of television credits, and recently launched the shipping of our desserts nationwide. Shoneji and I are excited to see where God takes us next! Most importantly our faith in God continues to grow. Even when things looked bleak, we knew God would not fail us and we're happy to report He hasn't. On our business cards it displays the bible verse Deuteronomy 28:4-6, 8, 11-13. When you're obedient blessings and God's favor will overwhelm you. It may not come easy each time, but just know they come. Things may come and go but the love of God lasts forever.

Day 4
Act As If It's Already Done

You need to act as if it is already done and just wait for the magic to happen.

SCRIPTURE

...Calls those things which do not exist as though they did.

ROMANS 4:17 (NKJV)

Today I'd like to tell you a funny story about how I once snuck into the BET Awards. I was still without a place of my own, and was sleeping on a girlfriend's floor. The day of the awards show, I told her I was going to attend. She asked me if I had tickets, and I simply replied, "No, but I'm dancing in the rain." I decided the easiest way to get in was by walking the red carpet just like the celebrities because no one was checking for tickets on the red carpet.

When we got to the red carpet, I heard someone call my name. I grabbed my girlfriend and told her that was our cue. I didn't know who had called my name at the time, but I knew it was now or never. Turns out it was Richard Butler, aka Rico Love, and he remembered me from our college days at FAMU. He invited us to walk the red carpet along with him and Usher. Usher grabbed my hand and off we went. When the paparazzi asked, "Who's the woman in the white dress?" I simpy waved and replied, "It's me!"

Once inside, my friend and I found two empty seats on the fifth row. We watched the entire show and had a blast. Now, I'm not sharing this story to encourage you to sneak into an event. I'm telling you this story so you will have a better understanding of how to apply the principle of acting as if it's already done. We were dressed to impress, acting as though we belonged there, and no one questioned us. Always remember that whatever it is that you're trying to achieve in life, you need to dress the part, act the part, and stay ready so you don't have to get ready. You need to act as if it is already done and just wait for the magic to happen.

PRAYER

Heavenly Father, I thank you for the power to call things that are not as though they were. I thank you because all things work together for my good. I ask for your divine intervention to be active and fulfilled in my life, to support the vision and the desires that you have given me. In Jesus' name, amen.

DECLARATIONS

To be recited out loud in front of the mirror with your right hand on your heart.

I WALK IN MY BLESSINGS.

I AM BOLD IN WHAT IS MINE.

I SEE OPPORTUNITY AND MOVE TOWARDS IT WITH GRACE.

I STAY READY SO I DON'T HAVE TO GET READY.

I AM FEARLESS IN PURSING MY DESTINY.

EXERCISE

What is something you need to face with boldness? In what ways can you prepare for what you believe God for? What's the one step toward what you believe God for you are going to do today?

FEARLESS FEMALE ENTREPRENEUR SPOTLIGHT

Kait Warman

Senior luxury fashion buyer, social media expert, blogger, speaker, podcaster

I love starting with introductions so, hey y'all! These days we are so used to connecting with people and barely knowing anything about them. And since I am talking about some things that are sensitive and quite near and dear to my heart, I want to start by at least telling you who I am.

So hey, I'm Kait. I am a city loving girl living in Los Angeles, constantly dreaming about Paris. I also happen to break out into dance whenever Celine Dion comes on. *Don't Judge.* I love almost nothing more than Disneyland. Everyone always asks me why. Well, I love it so much because it is a place where it doesn't matter what job title you have, or how much money you make, or even how old you are. No one uses big words. Everyone's smiling and joy filled. Your imagination is free to run wild. I honestly think Jesus would have spent a lot of time there.

Oh also, I am single, single as a dolla bill right over here (ha)! Here's the thing though...I used to so desperately want a boyfriend. Like so desperately. But honestly, all thanks to Jesus and His miraculous stedfast love, I have learned what loving all of myself was truly like. Not me plus one… just me. That one took some time. (more on this in a moment)

My walk with Jesus has been a rollercoaster of sorts to say the least! I guess the best way to describe it would be a wild ride that I have always stayed on, but that has definitely had its low and very weak moments of little faith. I grew up Catholic, in a unique Catholic church unlike many I have attended since. Our community was very tight knit and we often had the priests over for dinner. In high school I started going to a non-denominational church and absolutely loved it, though it very different from my formulaic Catholic roots. Experiencing worship like that opened my heart to feeling Jesus on a more personal level through music.

I would say in all honesty, though, that I was more of a believer than a true follower of Christ until I moved to NYC in 2012. It was here that I started to truly understand what a deep, loving relationship with Jesus was. I also learned what allowing the Holy Spirit into my heart truly meant. I was able to experience what abiding, dwelling, and delighting in His goodness truly looked like. How did I get to that place? Well, I have found that sometimes the best way Jesus really loves to emphasize his deep love and awaken us to it….is through deep times of pain and hardship. Not always, but sometimes. And least for me, that's how the narrative played out.

You know how above I mentioned that I was desperate for a boyfriend? Well, this desperation also meant that I sometimes got into relationships that I never should have be in. Or worse, was never supposed to stay in…*enter emotionally exhausting, utterly toxic, 2 and a half year relationship.*

Indeed, I met Jesus at this kind of a deep level in NYC while I was going through a relationship of deep havoc and turmoil. Emotionally, mentally, and physically it was a toxic relationship that sought to destroy every ounce of self love I had for myself, and it succeeded in many ways. I found myself broken, battered, shameful, and empty through that relationship (and believe me, I was no saint in it either). It was in that brokenness, when I had nothing else to cling to, that the Lord stretched out His arms and embraced me with His sweet love. It was a process, of rebuilding what was so lost in my heart. Of establishing a deep rooted foundation for myself. Of re-knowing who God said I was and who He had called me to be.

Since then it has been a waterfall of sweet, loving, glorious streams of love with the Lord. I would characterize my relationship with Jesus now as a sweet best friendship: the kind that I look forward to experiencing daily, and that I miss deeply when I put my own busy schedule above time with Him. Even though he brought me through that huge devastating relationship, I still am in need of His loving reminder of never failing grace… over and over and over, again.

We all have a story, but what I know more than ever is that the wounds of my past are not shameful scars. They are rather my victorious flags. Ones that I have spent time healing through and am now proud to claim freedom from. You might be thinking right now, what else makes my story what it is? There is not one easy way of putting it, but in short I have dealt with a variety of hardships including being in close proximity to drug addiction, being a victim of deception and betrayal, physical abuse, infidelity, sexual abuse, divorce, crippling anxiety, autoimmune disease, hormonal imbalances, and financial stress….to name a few.

Through all of this, though, what I believe is the greatest testament of them all is that I know none of the pain, heartbreak, stress, or confusion was without great gain. You see, I know that each and every part of my past plays an irreplaceable part in my current story. Each and every ounce of it contributes to the woman I am today, and the woman I am going to continue to grow into by His guidance. That is why I can sit here and write all of this to share with you today. I am not ashamed by the scars of my past, but rather excited to showcase them as badges of honor for what He has brought me through. Through each of these hardships the Lord has revealed Himself to me in deeper, sometimes unexplainable ways, and has immensely changed my life for the better…. all for His glory! On a personal level, friends, I just have to tell you all that I could not do anything in this life right now without 1) pursuing Jesus and opening my heart to His steadfast love daily and 2) my amazingly loving girlfriends, and wise mentors that help to champion me, love me, and bear with me through life's joys and trials 3) pouring out love and grace and kindness to others, just like Jesus does for me constantly.

Jesus has also been super faithful with the opportunities he has put in my life, too. I have been a senior luxury fashion buyer, a social media expert, a blogger, a speaker, and now a podcaster. I often have not felt worthy for these roles, but what I know is that God wants to take us to new and higher ground through empowering us and deepening his love in our minds, hearts and souls. My favorite parts of each day are the mornings when I get to soak in the new day, His new mercies, and the excitement for what is to come. So I want to leave you with these few questions.

How can you deepen a true and strong love for yourself that is rooted in the truths of God's goodness, steadfast care, and grace?

How can you lean on Him to bring you through trials and tribulations within the storms of life to bear witness for His glory? How can you own your story and wear your scars as badges of victory marked by the saving love and healing power of Jesus?

How can you use all of these things to impact those around you and see every opportunity to shower people with love and light and joy?

How can you empower others to know who they are, love themselves, and affirm them in their god given identities?

Live Loved,
Kait

Day 5
Your Focus

What you focus on expands.

SCRIPTURE

Finally, brothers and sisters, whatever is true, whatever is noble, whatever is right, whatever is pure, whatever is lovely, whatever is admirable—if anything is excellent or praiseworthy—think about such things.

PHILIPPIANS 4:8 (NIV)

What you focus on expands; it's a universal law. So much of life is about how you respond to it because your response and perspective will shape your reality. If you focus on complaining, God will bring you more things to complain about; if you focus on rejoicing, God will bring you more things to rejoice about.

That's why the above scripture says whatever is lovely, pure, and praiseworthy think about such things. If you focus on those things, you will receive more of that to focus on in your life. The mind is powerful, but please remember that it doesn't control your thoughts you do. If a negative thought enters your mind, delete it and replace it immediately with a positive thought. Make this your habit at all times.

I know life happens, and as a female entrepreneur, so many unexpected things can occur. Anytime I feel my energy shifting to a place I don't particularly care for, I immediately grab my journal. I write down a gratitude list of at least seven things I am grateful for and allow that list to be the focus of my day. I encourage you to do the same whenever you feel your attention shifting to something negative.

As it pertains to your focus, you hear me speak often in my talks about energy and energy management. Where attention goes, energy flows. There are certain situations that don't need your energy. Be mindful not to give attention to negative people, situations, or distractions, because once you do, you've wasted energy on something that will not serve your greater good. That energy could have been used to focus on positivity, prosperity, and productivity.

If you have a vision for your business and a team to assist you, you cannot spend your time working on a small task that should be delegated because it does not require your expertise. Now don't get me wrong, everyone starts somewhere and there was a day when you may have had to do everything by yourself to run your business. But in order to maintain growth and sustainability as your business blossoms, your energy is best used at the visionary level. Focus on your strengths and employ your weaknesses it's that simple. You will be more productive doing what you are best at versus spending your time on something you are not great at and producing a subpar product. This doesn't mean that you shouldn't step in to handle something that may need your attention from time to time. It does mean, however, that your focus needs to stay at a higher overview level.

Today I challenge you to be mindful of your focus so that you can get into the habit of focusing on that which fulfills you. When you make that shift, your life will be more fulfilled on a continuous basis.

PRAYER

Heavenly Father, Coming Messiah, I thank you that you have given us many wonderful things to focus on. Be a lamp unto my feet and a light unto my path. Show me the direction you would like to me go in. Show me how you would want me to spend my day so I can be the productive, prosperous vessel that you designed me to be. In Jesus' name, Amen.

DECLARATIONS

To be recited out loud in front of the mirror with your right hand on your heart.

I CHOOSE TO FOCUS ON WHAT FULFILLS MY LIFE.

I CHOOSE TO USE MY ENERGY WISELY.

I DEPOSIT THINGS INTO MY SPIRIT THAT ARE GOOD.

I FEED MY MIND WITH THINGS THAT ARE GOOD FOR MY SOUL.

I INCREASE MY INNER WORLD SO THAT MY OUTER WORLD INCREASES.

EXERCISES

1. Make a list of three things and find something negative about them. Analyze each one carefully. Then shift your focus by finding something positive about them.

2. Now that you have identified those three positive things. Create your own affirmations about them and recite each one three times.

FEARLESS FEMALE ENTREPRENEUR SPOTLIGHT

Monique Rodriguez

Owner of Mielle Organics

Mielle Organics founder and CEO, I have over nine years of experience as a registered nurse. My science background and focus on health from the inside out inspired me to share my regimen of healthy, tailbone-length hair with the masses. I started Mielle Organics 4 years ago after the loss of my son in 2013. I was pregnant with our 3rd child and the unthinkable happened. I had a uterine rupture and unfortunately my son was born lifeless. In order to keep my mental sanity I looked to my passion and started talking about hair care on social media and I started making products at home and talking about it on social media that was an outlet for me. My husband and I decided to get saved and surrender and give it all to God and that's when our life literally changed. Even though it's hard I'm at peace, a peace that surpasses all understanding. God has blessed me with a successful business so it's not my doing. I give all the glory and credit to our almighty God.

I'm passionate about inspiring women in business and entrepreneurship. While working as a nurse, I read multiple business books and considered my next career move. Daily, I imagined myself happy and fulfilled and ultimately working for myself.

I'm passionate about finding solutions to my own hair challenges, I began creating products in my kitchen and blogging about my hair journey on social media. I quickly gained traction, had an "aha moment," and the Mielle Organics journey began. I'm a very spiritual person who came to the realization that if God put the vision in me, then He'd equipped me with everything I needed to be successful. The business took off so quickly, that I started packaging products in my garage. My husband Melvin and I quickly became successful with launching Mielle Organics and the products are now sold in major retailers such as Sally Beauty, Target, and CVS.

Day 6
Built for Success

Fearfully and wonderfully made.

SCRIPTURE

What, then, shall we say in response to these things? If God is for us, who can be against us?

ROMANS 8:31 (NIV)

Above is a picture of the Saray Spa, located at the JW Marriott Marquis in Dubai. I always desired to go to Dubai but never verbalized it. So, imagine my surprise when the opportunity presented itself for my client, K Camp, to travel there on business. His manager, who also happened to be his mother, asked that I attend the trip as well. Of course, I jumped at the chance. I couldn't help but be amazed because you never know how God is going to manifest the desires of your heart. And while there, I had a spiritual awakening of sorts.

While at the spa, I enjoyed a beauty treatment where the water in the pool was directly from the Jordan River. I stepped into the water and as I tried to sit down, my body kept bouncing back up.

The Spa attendant working there asked: "Oh, you have never been in the Jordan?" I thought to myself, "Heck no, how is it that people just go to the Jordan?" She then informed me that the water in the river has such a high salt concentration that you automatically float. Just imagine being in water that you can't sink in…AMAZING. I have never witnessed being in water that pushed you to the TOP!

God was literally showing me, that when you lay in Him, He makes it impossible for you to fail, even if you try. There is no obstacle or situation in which God doesn't have your back. He has equipped you to succeed. He knew you before you entered your mother's womb. He crafted you to perfection. You are fearfully and wonderfully made. Ever wonder why when your skin is cut, it automatically heals itself? How awesome is that? Again, fearfully and wonderfully made. God's universe is so intricate in detail that it is designed to assist you in your success. The Jordan River is where Jesus was baptized. The Jordan flows all the way down into the Dead Sea and if you google it, you will see people floating on top of the water reading books and papers with no effort at all.

PRAYER

Father, I thank you for your creation. I thank you for creating something so marvelous that supports me in my success. I give you honor and glory. I praise your majesty. I thank you that I am fearfully and wonderfully made. In Jesus' name, amen.

DECLARATIONS

To be recited out loud in front of the mirror with your right hand on your heart.

I AM FEARFULLY AND WONDERFULLY MADE.

I AM DESIGNED FOR SUCCESS.

I AM BUILT TO SUCCEED.

GOD SUPPORTS MY SUCCESS.

GOD HAS A PLAN FOR MY LIFE.

EXERCISE

Write down three situations where God gave you the desires of your heart without you even asking for them.

FEARLESS FEMALE ENTREPRENEUR SPOTLIGHT

Brelyn Bowman

*Location Pastor for Spirit of Faith Christian Center's ECHO service,
Business owner, Author, TV show host*

I often take time to think about my life and the journey it took to get where I am because it keeps me grounded. The Brelyn Bowman that people see now has developed over time and I am simply amazed at how God has orchestrated my life. Most people think my life has been an easy ride because my parents are Apostle Mike and Dr. DeeDee Freeman, but like others, I had challenges, setbacks, and disappointments too. I made a lot of mistakes along the way despite my parent's guidance. Yes, I was a little stubborn and rebellious at times. However, I knew the voice of God at a very young age and made choices that kept me on track. I've always been driven, ambitious and a go-getter because I grew up in a loving home where I was free to express myself and be who God created me to be.

Though my parents valued my uniqueness, as the youngest of three children, I was a challenge for them because I always had my own ideas and didn't easily take no for an answer. However, they nurtured me and provided the guidance I needed to value myself and pursue and trust God with all my heart. As I approached my teenage years, I began to feel the demand on my life to go deeper with God and make him Lord of my life and not just savior. Trust God with all my heart. As I approached my teenage years, I began to feel the demand on my life to go deeper with God and make him Lord of my life and not just savior. I was internally compelled to live at a higher standard than what I saw in other kids my age without knowing my specific purpose and assignment.

When I understood that there was a spiritual call on my life to go into ministry, I took it seriously. I was so young, but I knew I had to make the right decisions because they were going to lead me to my purpose. So, I willingly committed my life to God beginning with my body. At 13 years old, I signed a purity contract with my parents that I would not have sex until I was married. It was a heavy commitment, but I knew that God was preparing me to serve him in a greater way. I was submitting to a desire that he placed in me to please him. By the time I met my husband, Tim Bowman, Jr. at age 18, I was still upholding the purity commitment I made to my parents and God, owned a brick and mortar fashion and accessories boutique, had written three books, and was a minister-in-training under my parents. Because I honored God for all those years, he has honored me by blessing me with a rare level of success for a person at my age. It blows my mind that now, at the age of 25, I'm a wife, minister, location pastor for Spirit of Faith Christian Center's ECHO service, business owner, author of six top-selling books, TV show host (The Tim and Brelyn Show), and founder of "Sisterhood", a women's organization designed to push other women into the next dimension of their lives. My life is continually blossoming as door after door opens creating new opportunities for me to expand the vision that God has placed in me. My life is purpose-driven. I don't move on anything unless I know it's from God and not Brelyn wanting to do something that just sounds good. I have learned "just because it's a good idea doesn't mean it's a God idea". I have followed this motto throughout my life and it has served me well.

After marrying my husband, my story of purity went viral. As a result, another door opened that I never imagined. We were blessed with a world-wide platform to share our story, two young adults just trying to live right. We had no idea of the responsibility we had when God brought our lives together. Following our appearance on Good Morning America, The View, Fox News, Yahoo, and many other television, websites and radio interviews, I began to receive countless invitations to speak all over the world to share my story and teach others how to live theirs within the guidelines of God's will. I now host an online "No Ring, No Ting" Bootcamp where I share a more in depth meaning of what it means to be pure. Purity is not a sex issue, it's a heart issue. I don't take any of this for granted. My success is in direct correlation with how I've honored God over the years. The commitment I made to God at just 13 years old was probably the most pivotal moment of my life because it set me on a path to where I am today.

Dreams do come true! I encourage you to live your dreams but follow God in the process. Someone is waiting on your yes! Your life is the greatest teaching tool. God doesn't give you the big picture of your purpose all at once, but I guarantee, you will not be disappointed by the outcome. I am living proof of that.

Day 7
Blessed to Be a Blessing

A man's gift makes room for him and brings him before great men.

SCRIPTURE

A man's gift maketh room for him, and bringeth him before great men.

PROVERBS 18:16 (KJV)

God has always blessed me by surrounding me with awesome people. One weekend, my girlfriend Cheryl Jackson treated me to car service, hotel accommodations, stellar meals and all around five-star service. I was in town to support her annual charity gala Feed Just One. Cheryl "Action" Jackson is the founder of the non-profit Minnie's Food Pantry. Her business and service is a testament to her life. Cheryl went from being homeless and hungry to feeding over 300,000 people through her organization. And that weekend, I remember thinking and praying to God that with all the people that Cheryl serves, this was my opportunity to be a blessing to her.

Proverbs 11:25 says, *"The generous man [is a source of blessing and] shall be prosperous and enriched, and he who waters will himself be watered [and reap the generosity he has sown]."*

As we prepped for the gala and assisted Cheryl in a production meeting, Regina King says: "Arian, call Will Packer. I know if you ask him for some premiere tickets to Think Like a Man Too for Cheryl to auction off for charity, he will say yes." I made the call and he said, "Sure!" They were auctioned off for $7000 to Tori Hunter of the Detroit Tigers. Not only was I happy that I could donate the tickets to benefit the gala, but I was even more excited to be able to bless my friend. From that encounter, I found other opportunities and experiences to be a blessing to her business.

God loves a cheerful giver.

2 CORINTHIANS 9:7

PRAYER

Heavenly Father, thank you for blessing me to be a blessing to others. Allow me to see opportunities to be a giver of the gifts you have given me. Direct me on where you want me to sow. In Jesus' name, Amen.

DECLARATIONS

To be recited out loud in front of the mirror with your right hand on your heart.

I AM BLESSED TO BE A BLESSING.

I AM A CHEERFUL GIVER.

I LIVE AN ABUNDANT LIFE.

MY CUP RUNNETH OVER.

I WALK IN THE OVERFLOW.

EXERCISE

Today, bless someone with the gifts that you have been given. If you are in the service business, offer someone a free service for the day. If you are in the product business, gift someone a free product. Find some way through your business to be a blessing to someone.

FEARLESS FEMALE ENTREPRENEUR SPOTLIGHT

Cheryl Jackson

Founder of Minnie's Food Pantry

As a child, I grew up on a street called Prosperity, where, ironically enough, prostitutes plied their trade on every corner. There were just as many vacant, rundown homes, and drug houses as there were inhabited ones. Living in a poverty-stricken area could be seen by some as one of the first challenges in my life, but with a mother and father who were both pastors, I was introduced to God very early on in life and knew without a shadow of a doubt that He loves me, and oh, how he loves me!!

It's not easy growing up in a household of nine. My parents were both givers and they would give (literally) our last to anyone in need. It didn't matter if it was food, clothing, furniture, if someone needed it-they gave it. Our home was built on a foundation of giving and it has since been instilled in me for nearly 50 years. It led me to start Minnie's Food Pantry 10 years ago in honor of the woman who gave her all; my mother, my pastor, and my best friend, Minnie Hawthorne-Ewing. When I started Minnie's Food Pantry, I didn't have the finances, connections or the man-power. I had something more valuable than the above. I had a whisper from God and I knew a few things:

(1) Many blessings come in disguise, It's God's way of showing us the full extent of His provision: Having married my high school sweetheart at just 17 years old, life has not always been easy. We were faced with hardships that lead to arguments that led to more hardships, which left us wondering if we made the right decision to get married so young. To say "we struggled" would be an understatement. Working 5 jobs collectively with two kids at home, and still unable to make ends-meet, it was hard to see the light at the end of the tunnel. Eviction after eviction. Living out of cars. Being turned away from assistance when we needed it most. Those were the early years...but God! He has a way of turning your pain into your passion. The negativity that we faced during our most vulnerable times left a permanent scar on my heart. A pain so deep that I didn't want for anyone to ever feel the disgrace and inferiority that I was faced with during my "rock bottom". I had to GROW through the pain of being treated "less-than" to see the silver lining. I vowed to create a sanctuary, a place of love, where we fill others up with dignity and serve with integrity. A safe-haven where people who need help can find it and help can find it and so much more! The struggle years-they were my blessing in disguise. They birthed the idea that flourished into what is now nationally known as Minnie's Food Pantry.

(2) When you are following the plan that God has designed for your life, your purpose is revealed and your dreams come true. I held onto faith and my life flip-turned upside down! Life got better, I built a successful career working for professional athletes, traveling the country making thousands of dollars a day. But there was this whisper in my heart that I couldn't shake. I toyed with it, thought on it but never acted upon it, until my father passed away. I was devastated and heartbroken. Having just lost the first man I ever loved, I became fearful of losing my mother too. I decided I wanted to honor her while I still could, and what better way than to build upon the whisper that I had been replaying over and over again for years. There was just one problem she didn't want me to. My mother pastored a church and as part of her ministry we operated Helen's House, a Food Pantry for our congregation in honor of her own mom. I've never

disobeyed my mother, after all she was the wind beneath my wings, but I felt in my heart it was time for me to soar, even if it meant going against her wishes. Fortunately, my mother has always been a woman after God's own heart and through fasting and praying, God showed her his vision and purpose for my life and gifted me what I had been yearning for her blessing.I learned that in order to walk in my destiny, I must first position myself to hear God's whisper, and then be strong enough in my faith to act upon it, despite the pushback, reminding myself that what is of God is already blessed!

(3) Love is the most profound gift I received/gave."Love is patient, love is kind. It does not envy, it does not boast, it is not proud. It does not dishonor others, it is not self-seeking, it is not easily angered, it keeps no record of wrongs." How can I truly serve another without love? I must always strive to be a prime example of love made visible. My actions should illustrate love and my words encompass it. I learned to love myself and others, in all that I do. I learned to see the beauty in every being. And I learned to love God who so passionately loves me, flaws and all. It's not so much what I do, it's the manner in which I do it which should always be with love, after all people will never forget how you made them feel!

My roadmap to success included several wrong turns and countless red-lights which taught me how to appreciate the detours in life, have unwavering faith in God's path he paved for me, as rocky as it might have seemed, and to love every stranger, every pit-stop, and every minute traveled. My destination: Minnie's Food Pantry, a nationally recognized non-profit organization thathas provided 8 million meals and counting to families in need. A top-rated organization that serves 60,000+ individuals annually and has been featured on The Food Network Chanel, Ellen DeGeneres show, Steve Harvey Show, Good Morning America and more. The #1 Charity in Dallas, TX, which has received the nod of approval from Hollywood elites including Oprah Winfrey, Mark Cuban, Roma Downey, Kevin Frazier, Floyd Mayweather and over 16,000 dedicated volunteers. But that's not all, stay tuned as I have yet to arrive at my final destination and there is so much more in store!

Day 8
God's Plan Always Prevails

Things are never falling apart; they are always falling into place.

SCRIPTURE

Many are the plans in a person's heart, but it is the Lord's purpose that prevails.

PROVERBS 19:21 (NIV)

When people hear my testimony, they often think it's a story about overcoming, and it is. It's also a story about being in alignment with God's purpose and plan; because when you are not, God often allows chaos to ensue, to get your attention, and to bring you into alignment with His plans.

I accepted a job after college because I was so exhausted from the ups and downs of entrepreneurship. As a college student, I owned a mall-based retail clothing store, which was rare for most college students. I had a lot of responsibility. I was paying my own bills, paying overhead on a business, enrolled in a 5-Year MBA program, a member of a sorority, involved in my community and more. I didn't have the maturity at that time to know that entrepreneurship has cycles. All I knew was I had this amazing grand opening for my store in the mall and then sales went down. But once the holiday came around, sales went back up, and then down again. Therefore, sometimes money was up, and sometimes money was down, which made me decide that I wanted something more secure, more stable. I wanted to know how much I had coming in each week, so that I could budget accordingly. I was getting ready to graduate, so I accepted the job with a steady paycheck. I truly believed that was the smart thing to do.

News flash: I worked that job for 30 days and got laid off. I couldn't believe it. I wanted something secure, something stable, and now my life was even less secure than it ever was when I owned the store. All I could ask was, "What just happened?" After losing my job, I was convinced everything was falling apart. I had multiple degrees, was a hard worker, yet I couldn't figure out why life wasn't working for me. I kept asking why. I'd done everything I was taught to do. The reality is that I was just simply born to be an entrepreneur; to run and own businesses. So, at this point in my life, it felt like everything was falling apart and working against me. Things started going left; I was onwelfare, receiving food stamps, and I was from a middle-class family. But then one day, it all started coming together again. I was given a chance to do PR and marketing work and I ended up with a business all over again. In the midst of me thinking that everything was falling apart, everything was actually falling into place. God was leading me back to the path of my destiny.

Confession: I never had days that bad when I owned the store. With all the ups and downs, they never got as low as they did after I was laid off. Now that I'm more mature and even more spiritually in tune, I understand that I was simply out of alignment of God's will. I was created to do business on this earth, and if I stay(ed) in my purpose, there will be ups and downs, but they will never be as bad as the moment that I stepped outside of what I was created to do.

Jeremiah 1:5 says: "Before I formed you in the womb I knew you, before you were born I set you apart." Being a business owner is who He created me to be. I couldn't run from it even if I tried. When I was homeless, I applied for over 153 jobs, but was never hired. God was clearly showing me His plan.

God created you for a reason and specific purpose. So even when you deviate from His plan, He uses your mess and works all things out for your good to bring you to where He wanted you in the first place. Remember, things are never falling apart; they are always falling into place. God's plan prevails; there is no need in fighting it. God gets us to where He wants us to be. Trust me when I say that it's never worth fighting God over your destiny.

When you go with God's plan for your life, life will be so much easier. You're more productive and fulfilled when you do what you're created to do. You produce better results for your life and for all the other people who you are assigned to, because they are also affected by all the wonderful things that you're doing. Strive to stay in alignment with your purpose because so many people are depending upon you to take your place.

It's ok if you mess up; I clearly did. You can always take your detour, but God will still get you to your destination.

PRAYER

Father, thank you for helping me trust your plans for me. It's my desire to be in your perfect will. Your ways are better than mine, so help me to stay in alignment and trust your path. In Jesus' name, Amen.

DECLARATIONS

To be recited out loud in front of the mirror with your right hand on your heart.

I KNOW THAT GOD HAS GREAT PLANS FOR ME.

I TRUST GOD'S PLAN.

I BELIEVE IN THE BEAUTY OF GOD'S PLAN.

I AM THANKFUL TO THE HOLY SPIRIT FOR GUIDANCE.

I KNOW ALL THINGS WORK TOGETHER FOR MY GOOD.

EXERCISE

Take time today to assess the beauty of God's plan. Journal your journey into adulthood and entrepreneurship. Write down how certain things were connected and led to other things. Be sure to list five things that led to moments in alignment with your destiny. Take time afterwards to thank God. Meditate on His goodness and marvel in His plan for your life.

FEARLESS FEMALE ENTREPRENEUR SPOTLIGHT

Jennifer Lucy Tyler

Modern Missionary & Soul Care Specialist

By 2004 I had dropped out of college, was broken due to toxic relationships and continued drug use, and had no sense of purpose or identity. In September of 2004 my best friend was murdered in a drive by shooting. It was there God met me. In my brokenness, and depression God pursued me relentlessly. I didn't find God because at the time I definitely was not looking for Him. He found me and began to speak to me. He started speaking to me in dreams and through other people. I would be somewhere I wasn't supposed to be and someone would randomly come up to me and say, "you don't look like you belong here, you are a woman of God." I started to have this sudden urge to read the Bible. When I began to pick it up, I couldn't put it down. I wanted to learn who God was, how I could be forgiven, and if He truly loved me. By July 2005, I stopped running, surrendered, and began to serve Him.

It was in Christ that my specific purpose was revealed. I knew that I enjoyed speaking. Even as a young girl I would be the one picked during school assemblies to speak. When I spoke I was confident and would own the stage. But now that I was an adult I wondered what would I speak about?

Who would listen? I started blogging my journey in 2004 and it was there I learned that I had an audience and became comfortable with sharing my story. In 2009, a well- known pastor's wife asked me to share my testimony in her book. After seeing the words of my story in its published form, I knew God wanted me to write to empower women. In 2011, my first book Dried Tears A Woman's Guide to Overcoming was released. I had no idea upon releasing this book the doors that it would open for my life. After its release I began to receive requests to speak all over the country. At the time I had to balance these requests with working as an Executive Assistant and absolutely hated having to say no to engagements. It was during that season when I discovered that I was not called to work in a traditional 9 to 5 work environment. Nonetheless, I was afraid to make the jump and valued the security a traditional job gave me. God has an interesting way of pushing us into our purpose even when we aren't trying. Over the next few years, every job I would work would either lay me off or let me go after 1 year. I was becoming known as the "lay-off" queen. In 2012 I was let go from what I thought was a "good government" job. But this time was different. I knew it was time to step out in faith and trust God with what was in my hand. I called my husband to pick me up and we discussed what I was sensing. We both had the peace of God and knew it was time for me to launch into the world of entrepreneurship.

October of 2012, on a beautiful autumn day I became a full time entrepreneur. I started out in the direct sales industry building my way up to a top-earner "millionaires" club position. This business gave me the freedom to develop my brand as a professional speaker, launch my non-profit, lead mission teams, preach the gospel and co-found an online boutique. None of this could be done without faith in a man greater than ourselves; and that man is Jesus Christ. Although, I had peace when I was let go from my job, fear was always a close lurker when things got tough. Launching out into the deep is always a scary thing. Life's waves can come crashing in at any time and it's those times we have to choose to either sink or swim in faith that God's got us. 6 years later those waves of life have come even harder as I endeavor to make greater impact in the lives of women and children globally. What keeps me grounded is the constant reminder of who God is and His sovereignty. Practically in order to keep this reminder before me, I have to keep His word in my heart. Prayer and bible study are a part of my daily "soul-care" routine. During the week I refrain from listening to music and listen to audio books and podcasts that help to keep my mind on Christ and to encourage my faith. I've recognized that God has opened the door for my success, and has added His super to my natural ability to serve a purpose that is greater than myself.

Day 9
Give God Room to Perform Miracles

If you have it all under control then what is the purpose of faith.

SCRIPTURE

Now to Him who is able to do exceedingly abundantly above all that we ask or think, according to the power that works in us, to Him be glory in the church by Christ Jesus to all generations, forever and ever. Amen.

EPHESIANS 3:20-21 (NJKV)

So often when running a business, there's a desire to be in control of everything--to be in control of every outcome. Sometimes we forget to leave room for God to perform miracles. When your hand is in every single thing and trying to control the outcome by doing this and that, you are telling God, "I don't need you to assist me in anything that I'm doing." We serve a God that's the God of the universe; He's in control of the universe. Wouldn't you want His help? Yes, faith without works is dead but we shouldn't be so in control that we obsess over outcomes. We need to leave some room for God to perform miracles in our lives.

Don't get so caught up on "I got to get this right and I have to perfect this, and I have to just get this to where the outcome looks just the way that I imagine." What if it's supposed to be greater than you imagined? What if it's supposed to be bigger than you ever dreamed? Ronne B., our female entrepreneur highlighted on this day, said the year she let go and let God she did $200,000 more in revenue over the previous year. She said she overworked before trying to control everything and realized sometimes we are just busy and not productive. Sometimes having your hands too involved in it, you're reducing the outcome of the magic that could just be. So just be mindful of that. If you have it all under control, then what is the purpose of faith? Leave some room for God to perform miracles in your life.

PRAYER

Dear Lord, I know your thoughts are above my thoughts and ways above my ways. I am excited, God, to create with you for I know that you do exceedingly abundantly above all that I ask, think or imagine. I marvel at your work and I look forward to all the miracles that you have in store for me. In Jesus' name, amen.

DECLARATIONS

To be recited out loud in front of the mirror with your right hand on your heart.

I WORK IN CO-CREATION WITH GOD.

I RELY ON THE HELP OF THE DIVINE.

I LISTEN TO THE HOLY SPIRIT.

ALL THINGS ARE POSSIBLE WITH GOD.

I EXPECT MIRACLES IN MY LIFE.

EXERCISE

Journal three things you are controlling tightly for which you can loosen the reins and surrender over to God. When you begin to obsess over the outcome, just say out loud, "Lord my trust is in you." As you release control and leave room for God to show up and show out, get ready for miracle. Walk in the spirit of confidence that all will work out beautifully. Walk in the spirit of expectation for you know great things are about to happen.

FEARLESS FEMALE ENTREPRENEUR SPOTLIGHT

Ronne B.

Coach, Author, Speaker, Entrepreneur

I am a wife, mother, coach, author, speaker, entrepreneur and overcomer. Yes that sounds like a lot, but I have influenced thousands of entrepreneurs by teaching them to achieve success on their own terms. My biggest goal is to inspire others to live and dream big.

I have worked very hard to change the trajectory of my life. I went from being a statistic to a success story. I know that God has used the obstacles in my life to show others that through Him all things are possible; be sure to trust the journey He has you on.

I worked long hours as a janitor while pregnant, but I didn't allow that obstacle to cause me to lose sight of my purpose. Even though the odds were stacked against me, I was determined not to allow my past circumstances to stop me from achieving my goals. After being laid off from my job with only an unemployment check as my income, and three children to care for, I knew I had to make a change. I was determined to face my fears, and step into my purpose. The lessons I learned on my journey as a teen mom gave me the courage to launch several business ventures.

In 2009, I founded High Heels High Goals, an exclusive, non-profit organization that teaches women how to be successful entrepreneurs and empowers them to reach their goals. Because I have a heart for women, on any given day you can find me pouring into the lives of other women by speaking positive words, sowing seeds to assist with start-up costs in a new business venture, or coaching a woman to success.

In 2014, I launched The Millionaire's Academy where I teach people all over the world how to leverage the direct sales industry and earn income from home. Through this program, I have helped men and women create six and seven figure incomes, become debt free, and live life on their own terms. My vision is to empower others to succeed in business, and inspire people to leave a legacy for generations to come. I coach entrepreneurs by using the strategies and methods I used to grow my own businesses as a leader. I believe success is no accident; if you want to achieve amazing things and build a successful business, you have to do it on purpose for a purpose.

Because of my obedience, hard work and dedication, I was able to turn a minimum wage income into a seven figure salary within a few short years. I achieved this goal without any formal training or business education. I am the face of success. Instead of focusing on fear, pain, and difficult days, I decided to endure and focus on the promise. When I am not coaching other women, leading seminars, writing or speaking, I enjoy spending time with my husband and our four children.

Day 10
Your Assignmentment

You are here to serve the people you are assigned to and anything above that is a gift.

FOCUS ON YOUR CALLING

SCRIPTURE

Well done, good and faithful servant! You have been faithful with a few things; I will put you in charge of many things. Come and share your master's happiness!

MATTHEW 25:23 (NIV)

I had the honor of speaking at Sophia Amoruso's Inaugural Girlboss Rally where I shared my journey and spoke on "7 Key Steps to Pursue Your

Dreams Fearlessly!" and it was a total success. The night before the rally, I attended the VIP dinner. I was seated next to Rachel Weiss, VP of Digital Innovation & Entrepreneurship at L'Oreal. She taught me a very valuable lesson at dinner: focus on your assignment and anything else you receive above that is a gift.

The rally was loaded with fabulous speakers and heavy hitters, such as Kevin Systrom, CEO and Co-Founder of Instagram; Susan Lyne, President and Founding Partner of BBG Ventures (and former CEO of Martha Stewart Living Omnimedia); Whitney Cummings; and more.

I wanted to see Gabrielle Bernstein's talk, but she was scheduled to speak at 9:15 a.m. and I didn't speak until 4:20 p.m. I explained to Rachel I was so upset that I was going to miss Gabby, and that I just didn't have time tomorrow to run back and forth along with getting ready. Rachel looked at me and said, "Arian we are not going to do this." She asked if it was best for me to run back and forth or was it best for me to get prepared on what I was assigned to do. I responded that it was best for me to get prepared on what I was assigned to do. She told me we are not going to have any FOMO (Fear of Missing Out) tomorrow. She repeated herself and said, "Look at me, no FOMO."

Rachel said, "You are here to serve the people you are assigned to and anything above that is a gift. And if you go into tomorrow with that attitude, there will be no lack, and you will be appreciative of all your gifts!"Rachel is honestly one of the coolest, sweetest people you would ever encounter. I was so glad she helped shift my perspective and got me "all the way together." I had to gift her a FEARLESS Shirt.
Though I didn't get to see Gabby speak, we still were able to connect and the timing was perfect. My day was filled with countless gifts and blessings, for which, I am more than grateful.

Hence my lesson to you is to stay focused on what you are called
Though I didn't get to see Gabby speak, we still were able to connect and the timing was perfect. My day was filled with countless gifts and bless-ings, for which, I am more than grateful.

SCRIPTURE

Well done, good and faithful servant! You have been faithful with a few things; I will put you in charge of many things. Come and share your master's happiness!

MATTHEW 25:23 (NIV)

PRAYER

Dear God, I know that you honor stewardship. Give me the guidance to always be responsible and accountable for that which you have given me. Show me how to manage and maintain what you have given me authority over, so that I stay focused on my assignment. I know when I do that, you will always provide more than I expected. In Jesus' name, amen.

DECLARATIONS

To be recited out loud in front of the mirror with your right hand on your heart.

I AM FOCUSED ON MY ASSISGNMENT.

I AM AN EXCELLENT STEWARD.

I AM DILIGENT.

I AM TRUSTWORTHY.

I AM RESPONSIBLE.

EXERCISE

For the next week, only focus on accomplishing three things each day and do those three things in the spirit of excellence. Because you are limited to doing only three things per day, you are focused on what matters to you the most for one week straight. Remember, where energy goes, attention flows. See what happens in your life when your energy is placed in the area of your assignment.

FEARLESS FEMALE ENTREPRENEUR SPOTLIGHT

Christina Murray

Realtor, CEO of Boss Lady Network, Business and Leadership Coach

My journey…well, what a journey it has been. At times, all I can do is laugh to keep from crying. My journey is ever-evolving. Where I stand today, is never where I imagined I would be, to say the least. I am forever grateful for every moment and every day that has been added, not just in my personal life, but in the growth of my business as well. There is a great quote that pretty much sums up everything: ***"No glass ceiling was ever shattered by a whiner."***

Let's start at the very beginning of my journey. My name is Christina Murray. I started out with a dream to go to college and get a degree in Physical Therapy. My parents were immigrants who came to the United States and worked so hard to build a life and career here. I grew up with a degree and career as my focus. Needless to say, being an entrepreneur was never in the equation. I was a very ambitious girl and a true leader at heart. Looking back, I do believe I was born with a special purpose, but life took me down a strange path to figure this out.

I got married at 18. Fresh out of high school, and my husband, Anthony, asked me to marry him on the side of Interstate 285 in Atlanta, GA. Now picture this—I'm married at 18 years old with my first child, and about to start college to jump start my American Dream. I know what you are probably thinking; I did it all backwards and yes, you are right. Fast forward 21 years and I am still married to the love of my life, Anthony. I have two super talented and amazing daughters, Jaseña and Jade. I would not have traded this part of my life for the world.

I began my real estate career about 17 years ago. I was not really interested in real estate at all, but my husband encouraged day after day to give it a shot. I could not grasp the idea of working for myself at all and I was never sure I could be successful at it. This is where the quote comes into play in my life. Things were pretty bad for us financially back then and I was living in frustration because I was young, with a family and no real career in place. I began to wonder, "Why me?" and "Will I ever be successful?"

For one to achieve greatness and success, it takes a different mindset and motivation. No one can change anything in their life by complaining about what is not right. I quickly realized that it was all or nothing. Shortly after I began my real estate career, my husband and I started our church, Oasis, in Paulding County. Again, having no clue and no direction, we went for it and have never looked back.

My real estate business had finally gotten off the ground and things were amazing. I was winning many awards and recognition in my company for its quick success and elevation. I was in the Million Dollar Club and loving my career. Our church was also growing faster than we could keep up. It grew in so many ways and many people were asking how in the world were we able to build such a vibrant ministry in the middle of a recession. Well, I trained hard, I worked hard, and I didn't look back. This brings me to a few years ago when I entered into another season in my life where I came to a crossroad as a business women and leader. WHAT NEXT? What happens when you get that sense that there is still more for you to do? You look past what you do every day and search for what you would want to do for a lifetime. You get to that place where your vision, purpose, and your destiny collide and you realize exactly where you need to be.

This is where I am today. I pushed through obstacles that didn't make sense or match up exactly with what I grew up envisioning.

There is what I like to call a, "Purpose Intervention." I learned a lot trying to build my career as a realtor and leader. I realized that if I could have had someone in my corner (besides my husband) helping and mentoring me, I could have gone even further. That is what led me to start the BossLady Network: a place for women in business to connect, network, and inspire one another. I learn every day something new and the fact that I get to share with so many talented and brilliant women each and every day puts the biggest smile on my face. I have an opportunity to coach and mentor new entrepreneurs, business women, and develop leaders and I couldn't ask for a better place to be in right now.

Don't get stuck on where you have been; always focus on where you are going. A glass ceiling is an unofficially placed barrier to keep you from advancement. It can never be shattered by whining, complaining, or using your circumstances to hinder your God-given greatness.
See you at the top!

Day 11
She Did What She Could

Vision and the Provision to Bring It to Fruition

SCRIPTURE

She did what she could.

MARK 14:8 (NIV)

I have always been a giver; it's one of my favorite things to do. Recently, I've become even more aware and intentional about giving to those around me. I was inspired by a video of a woman, LaDetra White, who went into her local barbeque restaurant and bought 100 meals. After watching this, I told God: "I would love to do something like that, it was so beautiful!" I told Him that I would love to give away a six-figure check to a business in need. God clearly spoke to me and said: "Arian, don't wait. Start now by using what you have." I always say when God gives me a vision, He will always give me the provision to bring it to fruition.

I was reading one morning in Mark 14 about the woman with the alabaster box which carried her most expensive bottle of perfume. She broke it and poured it on Jesus. That was her way of honoring Him. Some people tried to shut her down but in verse 8, Jesus spoke and said, "She did what she could."

People criticize celebrities by saying they have millions of dollars they should be giving to this cause or they need to support this, or they should be doing more to give back to their community. But the real question is, "Are you doing what you can?" For example, you may not be able to give on a level of a million-dollar donation, a hundred thousand-dollar donation or even a ten thousand-dollar donation; but are you giving the $10 to the person you see in need in a lunch line? Are you helping somebody else out with their small fee or an expense they may need help with?

There are so many people, and causes, who could benefit if we do what we can. No one is asking you to give or do anything beyond your ability. Don't ever put the pressure on yourself to do go above and beyond your means. Simply give from the heart whenever God leads you to be a blessing to someone in need.

So often people think they are operating from a deficit when they are not. God knows what you have. Philippians 4:19 reminds us that He provides all your needs according to his riches and glory through Christ Jesus. Too many times, people delay things because they think they can't get it done.

Anything that God wants you to do, He has already provided you with the means to get it done. God is not slothful concerning His promises. Start with what you have and let God do the rest.

MARK 14: 1-8 NIV

Now the Passover and the Festival of Unleavened Bread were only two days away, and the chief priests and the teachers of the law were scheming to arrest Jesus secretly and kill him. "But not during the festival," they said, "or the people may riot."

While he was in Bethany, reclining at the table in the home of Simon the Leper, a woman came with an alabaster jar of very expensive perfume, made of pure nard. She broke the jar and poured the perfume on his head.

Some of those present were saying indignantly to one another, "Why this waste of perfume? It could have been sold for more than a year's wages[a] and the money given to the poor." And they rebuked her harshly.

"Leave her alone," said Jesus. "Why are you bothering her? She has done a beautiful thing to me. The poor you will always have with you, [b] and you can help them any time you want. But you will not always have me. She did what she could. She poured perfume on my body beforehand to prepare for my burial.

PRAYER

Dear Heavenly Father, I am so thankful that you have given me all that I need and more. Guide me to who you want me to bless today. In Jesus' name, amen.

DECLARATIONS

To be recited out loud in front of the mirror with your right hand on your heart.

I AM A GIVER.

MY CUP RUNNETH OVER.

I TAKE JOY IN BLESSING OTHERS.

I AM BLESSED TO BE A BLESSING.

I DO WHAT I CAN WITH WHAT I HAVE.

EXERCISE

Today, I want you to be a blessing. You are being charged to give what you can. Whether you pay for a stranger's groceries, buy a coworker lunch, or simply write a friend a beautiful letter. Today is all about paying it forward.

FEARLESS FEMALE ENTREPRENEUR SPOTLIGHT

Pat Smith

Founder of P.S. by Pat Smith & Treasure You

As an entrepreneur, my greatest opportunities for growth have sprung from failure. Every, setback, misstep, and mistake has led me to right here. All along the way, God has held my hand, gently testing my knowledge and strengthening my faith. Every day as an entrepreneur, He has been my greatest asset. I just had to learn to listen and receive.

Throughout my entire adult life, my eyes were focused on a career in acting or broadcasting. I was knocked down more times than I can count, and dug in my heals with every rejection. In 2006, my husband Emmitt was a contestant on *Dancing with the Stars*, and while I was so happy for him, I wished I was the one on stage doing the samba. Emmitt won the Mirror Ball trophy that year and soon after I got a call to audition as the show's host. *It's finally my time!* I thought. I made it to the top three, but ultimately I didn't get selected to host. I was devastated. I prayed. I questioned God. And then, I let go. I knew that He was leading me through a season for a reason. And guess what? That pain caused me to search harder for my purpose, and it birthed a ministry and a business focused on helping other women.

Through my profound disappointment, God led me to the creation of my nonprofit, Treasure You. And through Treasure You I met incredible women who inspired me to write my first book, Second Chances. And that led me to the opportunity to launch my online boutique, P.S. by Pat Smith. And that led me to start writing my second book. And so on…

Today, thanks to my faith in God, I'm not fearful to start a new business, ministry, or nonprofit. I know that in the end it's all going to work out. God is by my side.

This doesn't mean you shouldn't be smart about what you take on. And, you must work hard. However, I'm always in prayer, asking God to let me know what He wants me to do. I listen. I take moments to be still. Although I network, make calls, and stay up day and night working on proposals, there is a time to be still. You have to find a good balance between the work you do and the quiet. You have to wait for God's direction. He's working on things that are greater than you think.

For example, I wanted to launch P.S. by Pat Smith about a year before it happened, but things weren't coming together. God was orchestrating the details and I had to be patient, even though I wanted it all right away! In the midst of my planning, my family was invited to participate on *Family Feud* and I questioned the timing. But there were signs from God that we should go to LA, and He was absolutely right! I used the flight to LA and fee we received from our appearance to invest in P.S. by Pat Smith … and the rest is history. That's what God does.

I learned to be patient so I could hear when He says go. When I felt that everything was lining up – the right people, the right support, the right moment – I could dive in with confidence and joy. And that's exactly what I felt when P.S. by Pat Smith went live. Joy.

I've learned that even if things don't work out the way I expect, it all still works out for His Glory. Being successful in business all comes down to faith. I no longer see setbacks as losses. Now, I look for the lesson. I live my life believing and standing on God's Word that all things work together. I ask God to show me the lesson and then I shift my business strategy to reflect those changes. After launching my store in the spring to near sell-out sales, I was worried because the summer is really slow. The old Pat would've questioned why. But today, I trust God's will.

As your faith grows, so do your business sensibilities, which then propels you even further. My relationship with God has grown through circumstances and struggles. I don't want to fail, and I don't want to disappoint someone (or myself), but things I don't like will happen. God uses setbacks to grow us up. Look to God and embrace your trials. He's got you. He's proven Himself over and over again.

Day 12
Stay in the Ring

If life knocks you down, just get back up.

SCRIPTURE

Now thanks be unto God, which always causeth us to triumph in Christ, and maketh manifest the savour of his knowledge by us in every place.

2 CORINTHIANS 2:14 (KJV)

The principle we are going to focus on today is staying in the ring. My girlfriend, Cheryl, once said to me "Arian, you always win." And I asked, "You know why? It's because I stay in the ring." If you're in a boxing match, you may get hit, you may get knocked down, you may even have a few scars in the end, but you should never leave the ring. The second you check out, you won't win the fight and life is all about fighting the good fight.

The reality is that things will happen unexpectedly, especially when you're running a business. You can encounter a little bit of anything and that's just what we call life. Just know that for every bruise, for every scar, it will all be worth it in the end. My great aunt Ossie always said, "Arian, if life knocks you down, just get back up." So, whatever it is you're going through, whatever it is you're dealing with, just remember to stay in the ring and keep fighting for what you want and deserve in life. If you stay in the ring, you can always compete to be the champion. There is a reward for staying power. When you stay in the ring you have tapped into the power of momentum. Because you choose to keep moving forward, doors will continue to open in the area that you are working in. I am telling you from experience that if you slow down, things around you slow down too. God is responding to your pace. This is also why progress and completing a goal, is better than perfecting something, because you are continuously moving. People are attracted to you when they see you are working towards a goal; others want to join in on it too. When it comes to being persistent in pursuing your dreams, you must make sure you speak to the right people and ask the right questions. I remember when I was building my business back in 2004. I knew that if I asked questions and got a "no" while recruiting clients, I either asked the wrong question or spoke to the wrong person. I only dealt in yes.

For example, say you have a flight issue and you call Delta Airlines and speak with the first representative who happens to answer the phone. And you keep getting a no about whatever it is you want to get done. You may want to ask to speak with their supervisor. This isn't to say that the person who answered the phone isn't competent, but that person may not be in a position of authority to give you a "yes." Always speak to people with the authority to give you a "yes." You may need to rephrase your question or ask that same question to someone who is in a higher position. Just remember that if you're getting a no, you're either talking to the wrong person or you're asking the wrong question. Always stay in the ring, because there is a false sense of peace that comes with quitting. Don't quit. Adjust and keep it moving. The victory is yours!

PRAYER

Dear God, I want to thank you that you have called us to be more than conquerors! I give you glory, honor, and praise for your plan is perfect. I know that I can do all things through Jesus Christ who gives me strength. I am so grateful that no weapon formed against me shall prosper, and Lord, I thank you for every victory in advance. In Jesus' name, amen.

DECLARATIONS

To be recited out loud in front of the mirror with your right hand on your heart.

I HAVE POWER.

I AM PERSISTENT IN MY CALLING.

I AM MORE THAN A CONQUEROR.

I HAVE DOMINION AND AUTHORITY.

I HAVE THE VICTORY IN EVERY AREA OF MY LIFE.

EXERCISE

Write down three adjustments you can make in your business before you give up on a goal. And if you aren't about to give up on a goal, still write down three adjustments you can make in your business that will directly increase your bottom line.

FEARLESS FEMALE ENTREPRENEUR SPOTLIGHT

Kirsten Grove

Interior Stylist and Author

As an interior stylist and author I've had a passion for interior design since I was nine years old and given free reign over decorating my bedroom. Back then, I chose an eclectic palette of rainbows, polka dots, and stripes. I also created zones in my bedroom which included a reading zone, playing zone and sleeping zone.My friends always got annoyed with this arrangement, but it never stopped me from doing my own thing.

Growing up in a Christian home, I experienced Jesus first hand as a young child. I quickly learned through traumatic moments and hard seasons that God was faithful and that he would never leave me nor forsake me. When I was just 12 years old, I went through two major surgeries that left me without ovaries. This could have created insecurities and deep sadness in my life, but because I had a relationship with my heavenly father, I took these circumstances and used them for God's glory.

Today, I reside in Boise, Idaho with my husband and two adopted children.

Both of my children have amazing stories of their own, and both are little advocates for adoption. Because God used adoption so strongly in their lives, my children hope to spread the news about the importance of adoption.

I use my platform as a designer to create beauty out of barrenness, both practically and spiritually. Simply Grove Blog has become a hang-out for like-minded creatives with a love of interiors and an appetite for design eye-candy. I have been featured in publications and sites such as Sunset Magazine, LA Times, Family Circle, Architectural Digest, My Domaine, Lonny Magazine, Marthastewart.com, Better Homes and Gardens, HGTV.com, Domino.com, and Design* Sponge. I recently released my first book, Simply Styling, which showcases simple, yet beautiful design that is achievable and budget-friendly.

Day 13
Busi-Ness vs. Business

What Are You Producing?

SCRIPTURE

"Martha, Martha," the Lord answered, "You are worried and upset about many things, but few things are needed—or indeed only one. Mary has chosen what is better, and it will not be taken away from her."

LUKE 10: 41–42 (NIV)

Do you know the difference between being busy and handling business? Because there is a difference, and right now we live in a very busy, driven society. Honestly, some of it just has to stop in order for us to fulfill our purpose. I'll never forget, when I started Fearless Magazine and people asked me, "Oh, what else do you have going on business wise?" I had a magazine that was nationally and internationally distributed and in every single Borders and Barnes & Noble and they had the nerve to ask me what else I was doing. So often, people put so many pressures on us to just be busy. To publish a magazine was such a huge undertaking that I couldn't understand why people asked what else I was working on.

People are so caught up in what you are doing, but the real question is what are you producing? Whatever work you do needs to be something that affects the bottom line or the productivity of the company. We already know that we're to be fruitful and multiply, therefore you need to be producing something. The other day, I looked at my old motto from my school of business industry at Florida A&M University and I just cracked up. My dean hit the nail on the head with this motto for the business school: "No excuse is acceptable; no amount of effort is adequate until proven effective."

We get caught up in many tasks that just keep us busy when we could actually save some time by sitting, being present, and focusing on the tasks that will move our business forward. It's called focused energy. When my sister Ashley was stationed in the UK for work, she learned a very valuable lesson about this very topic. She was concerned that the CEO of her company would be upset with the culture of the new company he'd just acquired. You see, employees arrived around 10AM, took a break for high tea and lunch, and when the work day was over, they did not take phone calls outside of work hours. I then explained to Ashley that the employees were simply focusing their energy and because they had assigned social time and assigned work time, they were able to focus on the task at hand. Their productivity allowed for the company to be profitable while they enjoyed the benefit of being fully present in each moment. I am more than grateful for my upbringing, but in high school I was overly involved. I was an honor roll student with a 3.9 GPA, a cheerleader, a member of a professional dance company, a student council member and more. Plus, I held down two jobs. When I got to college, I continued to be overly involved. I pledged Delta, was in student government, volunteered within the community, and owned a clothing store in the mall. However, I now realize that college itself should have been enough for me.

I'm pretty sure some of you have heard the story in Luke 10:38-42 NIV about Mary and Martha. When Jesus went to Mary's house, Martha occupied herself by being busy.

As Jesus and his disciples were on their way, he came to a village where a woman named Martha opened her home to him. She had a sister called Mary, who sat at the Lord's feet listening to what he said. But Martha was distracted by all the preparations that had to be made. She came to him and asked, "Lord, don't you care that my sister has left me to do the work by myself? Tell her to help me!"

"Martha, Martha," the Lord answered, "You are worried and upset about many things, but few things are needed—or indeed only one. Mary has chosen what is better, and it will not be taken away from her."

You don't always have to doing something just for the sake of having something to do. Honestly, some of it is not even productive. You're just occupying your time. Be mindful that you're not in the habit of being busy when there is more value in sitting still and bring present.

PRAYER

Dear God, give me the guidance to focus on that which is productive as my goal is to be fruitful and multiply as you have instructed. I choose to seek ye first the kingdom and all things shall be added. Lord, bless me with divine wisdom and strategy as I journey on with my day. In Jesus' name, amen.

DECLARATIONS

To be recited out loud in front of the mirror with your right hand on your heart.

I AM FOCUSED.

I AM PRODUCTIVE.

I HANDLE TASKS EFFECTIVELY.

I REST WHEN I AM SUPPOSED TO REST.

I WORK WHEN I AM SUPPOSED TO WORK.

EXERCISE

If you make a to-do list, which I am sure you do, remove three things off your to-do list and see how the day goes. If you find you have free time, DO NOT add those things back to your list. Simply enjoy your free time as you go about your day.

FEARLESS FEMALE ENTREPRENEUR SPOTLIGHT

Tori Bolt

Bolt Farm Treehouse

I quit my job in broadcast news in January 2017 to work for myself and to help grow my family's business. A few years ago, my husband built a luxury treehouse in Walhalla, SC with his dad. At first, it was just to have a peaceful place to disconnect from the busy world and find deep rest, but it wasn't long until they realized thousands of others were seeking that same rest and most were long overdue. They opened Bolt Farm Treehouse to the public through Airbnb in October 2015 and immediately experienced rapid growth. I was working at NBC news in Charleston at the time running the station's web and social media sites, in addition to entertainment reporting. In my free time, I used my skill set to do social media marketing for the treehouse but had very little time and energy to do it all. I felt conflicted because my heart was in growing the treehouse business, but I had to give it my leftovers after my nine-hour shift (plus hour commute) at the news station.

That's when I realized I would much rather work for myself and invest my time and energy in what I'm truly passionate about, versus having job security and a bi-weekly direct deposit check from a corporation. Leaving my job in news was no easy decision and it took a lot of faith, but I believe God honors us when we act in faith. Having all the answers doesn't require any faith. Boldly stepping into the unknown, relying on God's direction does. It requires more faith than we are usually comfortable with, but that's where things get exciting.

Now I use my talents as the public relations and social media marketing director at Bolt Farm Treehouse. I've watched us grow from 150 followers on Instagram, to more than 15,000 in less than a year. I have also helped us land national features including on the TLC network. I work hard to make sure our treehouse is getting good media coverage, staying connected on social media, finding collaborative opportunities, and continually improving the guest experience as we implement new ideas. Each work day is different, and every day presents new challenges, but it is always rewarding.

My hope is that each person who walks through those antique treehouse doors experiences true rest and basks in God's presence. I've found that I can hear God's voice most clearly when I quiet all the outside noise and spend time with Him—without being rushed or having my thoughts consumed with the rest of the day. One of my favorite things is reading the guestbook entries and hearing about how our guests felt God's presence and peace at the treehouse. Some share how their marriage relationship was restored. Others left refreshed, renewed and ready to enter their regular modern life with a new mindset and appreciation for nature.

Being an entrepreneur gives you the ability to work without any ceilings placed upon you, and do what you enjoy. However, it also requires you to rely on God for help and guidance every day. Our ideas, plans and desires are finite, but God's plans and desires, have no limits. It's only when we surrender our plans and dreams to Him do we remove those low ceilings. Whatever you want to do, you can do it with His help.

Day 14
Fear of the Unknown

If you know everything then where does your faith come in?

SCRIPTURE

For I know the plans I have for you," declares the LORD, "plans to prosper you and not to harm you, plans to give you hope and a future.

JEREMIAH 29:11 (NIV)

Never fear the unknown. So often people get worked up with fear of the unknown. It may be a business venture you're scared to leave because you fear what the future may hold without it. Or it may be a business relationship you're scared to leave because you think you need it to achieve some success. The fear of the unknown needs to be eliminated.

What God has for you is already done. He predestined it before you entered your mother's womb. We must cast fear out completely and quickly. So many people think they are bound to certain people, things, and situations because they fear the unknown. Often, people get anxious and anxiety is nothing but worrying about something that hasn't happened yet. You're worried about something that hasn't even taken place yet. There is no need to worry about that.

And there's no need to fear the unknown; the unknown is not going to kill you. Get up the next day, approach it with grace, courage, and fearlessness. There is no need to fear the unknown. And starting today, we're going to stop all of that. If a negative thought comes to mind, replace it with a positive thought immediately. Don't let stress steal your joy. Stress isn't real. It's simply a coping mechanism people choose to adopt when they are facing the unknown. We serve an all-knowing God who has great plans for us. There's no need to fear the unknown. If you know everything, then where does your faith come in?

PRAYER

Dear Heavenly Father, I am so grateful that I serve an all-knowing God. I am thankful that Your yoke is easy and Your burden is light. I cast all my cares on you and move forward with excitement and joy about all the wonderful things you have in store for me. In Jesus' name, Amen.

DECLARATIONS

To be recited out loud in front of the mirror with your right hand on your heart.

I SERVE AN ALL-KNOWING GOD.

I SERVE A GOD WHO MAKES NO MISTAKES.

I SERVE A GOD WHO HAS GREAT PLANS FOR ME.

I SERVE A GOD WHO HAS PREDESTINED ME TO SUCCEED.

MY GOD WORKS ALL THINGS TOGETHER FOR MY GOOD.

EXERCISE

Think of three times when you got nervous about an outcome and God showed Himself to be faithful. You weren't taken out then, and any obstacle you are currently facing won't take you out now. Write down the victorious outcome of those three times where you had anxiety and everything worked out better than you imagined. Reflect on this.

FEARLESS FEMALE ENTREPRENEUR SPOTLIGHT

Nichole Lynel

CEO & Creative Designer at Shop Nichole Lynel

Two and a half years ago, prior to launching my online fashion business, I was far from the fearless fashionista I am today. I knew where I wanted to be but I had no clue on how to get there. I knew God had a big purpose for me but I was so crippled by fear and doubt I always questioned "The Call."

The one thing I did know for certain was that I am a fashion girl—from my first set of Chanel paper dolls at five, to the way my soul lit up sneaking into my aunt's mink coat and matching hat. Fashion gave me life. But in my house, I was taught fashion was a hobby just for fun, not an option for a career. My entire life, I have been praised for my fashion sense and my eye for beauty. But I ignored the thing that made people stop me on the street.

I was a sheep just shuffling through life doing whatever job was suggested. You name it: modeling, teaching, photography, retail. Each and every day, I felt like God must have more for me.

Then finally He heard me. Right before my 30th birthday, I prayed and it was an ugly-cry prayer. I vowed that if I could just get the chance, I would do the work. Then boom! Just like that, I made the decision. I was not put here to be mediocre. That little whisper grew loud and drowned out my doubts and fears. I totally heard, "If you build it, they will come." I began doing the work I was destined to do.

You see, I truly believe that when God wants a change he will make you very uncomfortable. It was all on purpose. All those jobs were in preparation for where he was taking me! So please never doubt the process. He is working things out in your favor. He always has been and always will be. Even when it seems bad it's good because God is good!

Fashion was just the beginning for me and I want to encourage you to follow your dreams, because with God, anything is possible.

Day 15
Process to Promise

Don't fight the process, trust the process, and most importantly, enjoy the process!

SCRIPTURE

But let patience have its perfect work, that you may be perfect and complete, lacking nothing.

JAMES 1:4 (NKJV)

Today, I want to discuss the process of pursing your purpose and God's promise. And Lord have mercy, I wish somebody would have taught me this at a very early age. When I was in my early twenties and owned my own mall-based retail store, I can honestly say I just didn't have patience. I wanted the promise, but I didn't want the process. However, the reality is that there is a process that must take place to get to the promise land. That's why people tell you to enjoy the journey and not just the destination.

There's so much that goes into the process that may not look the way we want it to look. If somebody told me that I was going to be travelling the world doing tour publicity for Chris Brown and working on blockbuster movie hits, I would have said, "Sign me up!" But, had they told me that before all my success, that I was going to end up homeless and living out of my car, selling my clothes just to eat and put gas in the car, and surviving off food stamps, I would have said, "You all can have the tour. You all can have these number one movies. You can keep all that extra stuff because I don't want to go through that."

When people hear my testimony, I tell them all the time that it was clearly nothing but God, because I would've written an entirely different script. But then I would have further delayed my destiny of getting to the promise because of all that I had to go through during the process. Therefore be patient as you go through the process. It's just life. Things just happen. Be willing to enjoy the journey while you get to the destination. It's a marathon, not a sprint. You must go through the process to get to the promise. I need to make this disclaimer: process doesn't mean struggle nor does process mean pain; it just means process. I don't want anyone thinking their process must look a certain way to get to what they desire. It's not God's desire that we struggle, we serve a loving God. It's the caterpillar to the butterfly; it's the cake ingredients to the full baked cake.

I interrupted my process when I left my store to go get a job and caused disruption in my life. God was already working on my patience with the store, but I didn't like how it looked. When I took matters into my own hands, things got worse because God was trying to increase my character. He took my mess and still increased my character since that was His plan all along. He took my detour and still got me to my destination. Don't fight the process, trust the process—and most importantly, enjoy the process.

PRAYER

Lord, guide me and teach me to have patience in the process, for I know the process is building my character to sustain the promise. Lord, prepare me for the promise that I am praying for. In Jesus' name, amen.

DECLARATIONS

To be recited out loud in front of the mirror with your right hand on your heart.

I ENJOY LIFE.

I AM PATIENT.

I SEE BEAUTY IN ALL THINGS BIG AND SMALL.

I EXPECT AND RECEIVE EVERY BLESSING GOD HAS FOR ME.

I SEEK TO OPERATE AND BE THE BEST AND HIGHEST VERSION OF MYSELF.

EXERCISE

Journal three things you desire right now and write down what you will gain if you allow God to perform His perfect work in you.

FEARLESS FEMALE ENTREPRENEUR SPOTLIGHT

Jasmine Star

Photographer, Branding + Marketing Strategist

For as long as I can remember, Sunday school was a part of my life. I sang songs out of tune, I carried a picture Bible, and ate graham crackers and punch after each teaching. I memorized scriptures, I attended vacation Bible school, and I went to church camp.

Basically, I was a typical Christian kid growing up in Southern California. But something happened that radically changed my life. No, scratch that. A lot of somethings happened to change my life.

- My parents lost their home when they couldn't pay their mortgage.
- We were the recipients of government-issued food and church donations.
- My dad's car couldn't start on its own, so every morning his five kids pushed it down the street to jump-start the engine.
- I was an obese child and endured an eating disorder when I was 13 years old in attempts to lose weight.
- My grandmother passed away in my arms.

- My mother was diagnosed with brain cancer.
- I dropped out of law school.

The list went on and on, but this story isn't about me. This testimony is about God's goodness in my life. There were times when I begged God to change my life, to alter my circumstances so I wouldn't have to face the pain of my journey. More often than not, I was met with divine silence.

It was in God's silence that He showed me His undying love. It was in God's silence that I witnessed miracles. It was in God's silence when I learned to trust His will, not mine.

I've slowly learned that God is shaping my story with each passing trial to prove His goodness and mercy. My testimony is filled with endless stories of the Lord never leaving my side. God walked with me. God walks with me. God will continue to walk by my side in order for me to pursue the upward calling of Christ.

Day 16
You Have What You Need

Whatever it is that you have right now, you can do magnificent things with.

SCRIPTURE

But my God shall supply all your needs according to his riches in glory by Christ Jesus.

PHILIPPIANS 4:19 (KJV)

All that you need, you already have. The Bible says that God supplies all our needs according to his riches in glory through Christ Jesus. Often, people think they're operating from a deficit, but anything that you need to get done at this moment, you already have.

When speaking to today's youth, every now and then there is a young child who thinks they are missing something because they may be in a single-parent household or a similar situation. I look at them and tell them, "This may be hard for you to understand now, but the reality is, if you needed it to do what God wants you to do, God would have supplied it." You actually have what you need in order to do whatever it is that God has called you to do. You're not working from a deficit.

I know a story that everyone can relate to. Have you ever gone to the grocery store only to return home having purchased something that you already had in your house? I think we are all guilty of this at some time in our life. It's because we didn't take inventory of what we already had before we went shopping. We do this in business too. We go out looking for people and resources to assist our business. If we just took inventory, we would see which resources already exist in our current network.

Whatever it is that you have right now, you can do magnificent things with. Don't worry about what you don't have because remember, I've said it before, what you focus on expands. You need to be in the mindset of abundance at all times. Remember that you already have what you need.

PRAYER

Dear God, I thank You for all that You have supplied me with according to Your riches in glory through Christ Jesus. I thank You for the abundance that You have given me. Lord, lead me in the right way to maximize and multiply all You have blessed me with. In Jesus' name, amen.

DECLARATIONS

To be recited out load in front of the mirror with your right hand on your heart.

I AM FULLY EQUIPPED.

GOD SUPPLIES ALL MY NEEDS.

I MAXIMIZE THAT WHICH I HAVE.

MY NEEDS AND WANTS ARE MET.

EXERCISE

The exercise today is to take inventory. Take inventory of all of your resources. If you are raising money for a non-profit, write out a list of potential donors already in your immediate reach. If you need help with marketing and/or operations, do the same thing. God has already provided you with everything and everyone to meet your current need.

FEARLESS FEMALE ENTREPRENEUR SPOTLIGHT

Julie Solomon

Marketer, Influencer, Author, Podcaster

I grew up in a Christian family, so I was surrounded by God and the church from the very beginning. I was raised in a Christian home, but as I got older I just followed the motions of doing "Christian things" that I thought you were supposed to do. I didn't know Him, I just knew about Him.

I found myself searching for purpose and meaning in people and also in myself. Whether that was my friends or in relationships, I poured my whole heart into them. I also became very fixated on myself and the world around me. I became very consumed with what people thought and was living for the acceptance of the world.

When I was at my lowest point was when I knew I needed to surrender. From growing up in a Christian home, I knew what to do. I knew that He could save me if I just let Him. That is when I committed to service and I committed to living for God instead of others. And that is when my business completely changed. It became about something bigger than myself. God shows me every day that being a "Christian" isn't about just doing good works. He made it clear that I do not have to earn my salvation or His love. I have it from and by his grace. He has given me fulfillment and purpose and joy that I am able to now share through my business and my community.

I am not perfect and I still mess up, but God loves me despite my flaws and imperfections. Having this belief at my core allows me to have and grow in faith while maintaining a successful business.

Be still and know...

Day 17
Team Building

You want to hire people for where you're going not for where you're at.

SCRIPTURE

Both you and these people who are with you will surely wear yourselves out. For this thing is too much for you; you are not able to perform it by yourself. Listen now to my voice; I will give you counsel, and God will be with you.

EXODUS 18:18-19 (NKJV)

Building the ideal team for your dream is so important. Your dream should be so big that you need the help of others. When people are building their teams especially those who are starting out, you start hiring people and paying people according to what you can afford. But news flash: that's not always good. You want to hire people for where you're going, not for where you're at.

I'm going to explain how you can effectively build your dream team. I know your first thoughts are, "What if I don't have the cash?" It's not about the money, it's about the sourcing. Get people who are on the executive level, who have big visions. Ask them to volunteer their time, even if it's simply one hour a week or a month. One hour of their time can be of better use than somebody who's just working $10/hour simply maintaining something for you. The wisdom and the expertise of that person giving an hour of their time is priceless. And guess what, over time, they may keep volunteering; and you'll start making more money. Eventually, you'll be able to pay them and you'll be able to hire them. During that time of growth, you're able to adopt and use all of their wisdom and skill set everything that they bring to the table. However, keep in mind that during that time you were paying someone what you can afford, you may never even grow. Instead, now that you have gone big, you're increasing your potential for growth. So when it comes to building your team, go for the top, shoot for the stars, don't hold back, go big. Jesus is the best example for how this can be done. When he set out to choose his disciples, he selected people who were already doing business. He built his team with executive level people. People who had skills sets. People who had experience. People who were useful for his purpose and ministry.

From my personal life experiences, I have also noticed that when I do His work, God sends His people. It's so amazing when God gives you different visions to work on. He already has the provisions, which include the people that will want to help with your project. Anytime you start something of great magnitude, people will be drawn to greatness. Every time I get ready to start a huge venture, people come from everywhere asking if they can help by volunteering to be a part of a Fearless Discussion or by doing something for my Business Club. Now don't get me wrong; you can't take everyone's help who offers it. Still there are people who will be sent to you with the right skill set you actually need. However, this does not mean you sit around waiting for people to come to you. You should still source great talent, but because you are doing His work, his doors will open to you.

Reality is that you need help with your dream. Moses faced a challenge we see in today's scripture. If he didn't have the proper help, he would have worn himself out. I am sure many can relate. Read the passage below where he receives instructions from his father-in-law on how to delegate responsibility.

So Moses' father-in-law said to him, "The thing that you do is not good. Both you and these people who are with you will surely wear yourselves out. For this thing is too much for you; you are not able to perform it by yourself. Listen now to my voice; I will give you counsel, and God will be with you: Stand before God for the people, so that you may bring the difficulties to God. And you shall teach them the statutes and the laws, and show them the way in which they must walk and the work they must do. Moreover you shall select from all the people able men, such as fear God, men of truth, hating covetousness; and place such over them to be rulers of thousands, rulers of hundreds, rulers of fifties, and rulers of tens. And let them judge the people at all times. Then it will be that every great matter they shall bring to you, but every small matter they themselves shall judge. So it will be easier for you, for they will bear the burden with you. If you do this thing, and God so commands you, then you will be able to endure, and all this people will also go to their place in peace."

EXODUS 18: 17-23 (NKJV)

PRAYER

Dear God, thank you for blessing me with a great vision. Thank you for being so mindful of me that you give me the desires of my heart. I trust you to bring every person and resource needed in order to fully manifest your vision. In Jesus' name, amen.

DECLARATIONS

To be recited out loud in front of the mirror with your right hand on your heart.

I THINK BIG.

I OPERATE ON THE LEVEL OF MY VISION.

GOD SUPPLIES THE PROVISION FOR HIS VISION.

I HAVE EXCELLENT RESOURCES ALL AROUND ME.

I HAVE THE RIGHT TEAM FOR MY DREAM.

EXERCISE

Think about the vision for your company. Are there any positions that you need filled to make your vision a reality? Write out 10 potential prospects for that position. Reach out to those potential prospects and share your vision with them. If you are not in position to hire them at the moment, see if they are able to volunteer, are a good fit and willing to support the vision.

FEARLESS FEMALE ENTREPRENEUR SPOTLIGHT

Dr. Kym Lee-King

Minister. Mom, MUA, & Motivator

I am a faith focused beauty-preneuer, and I believe that faith is the key ingredient in all successful settings. Whether you're an entrepreneur or working in at a fortune 500 company, this current economy requires that the people of God honor Him in our business practices by seeking direction in our pathway to success. But there is more to "Success" than merely following godly principles. The Bible describes it like this in Matthew 17:20

Truly I tell you, if you have faith as small as a mustard seed, you can say to this mountain, 'Move from here to there,' and it will move. Nothing will be impossible for you." So, am I suggesting that it's more than skills and hard work...? The answer is yes!

As a 25-year celebrity MUA, Minister, and beauty motivator, I've experienced the ebb and flow of success both financially and spiritually. And my lowest moments were typically due to a lack of faith. I've learned that it's important to maintain a connection to my source for wisdom, strategy, and guidance. But the big steps in these areas required big faith!

And that is the substance of things hoped for with no evidence or visual manifestation! So, yes I'm challenging you to step out into an area you are unfamiliar with believing that God will guide you and giveyou the wisdom to achieve your next set of goals! Just like He did for me when I decided to leave Georgetown Law School to peruse a career in beauty. I left what was comfortable and sure to peruse the unknown. I desperately wanted my passion to meet my purpose in life.

And that leap of faith opened up doors that most make-up artists only dream of. For over 2 decades I've been blessed to work on movie sets with A-listers, like Angela Bassett, Kerry Washington, and Forest Whittaker...

To sit courtside at Wimbleton with the world's best tennis players, Venus and Serena Williams; to speak on major platforms like the Potters House with Serita Jakes, and even into the White House with former presidential candidate Hillary Rodman Clinton.

Sis... just like me you've done the work, you've studied the craft, and made the connections... so what's blocking you from those open doors? I would venture to say it's your lack of faith! It's time to believe... Don't just feed your career goals while starving your faith! Your faith is the nutrient needed for your growth! Speak it into existence ... it belongs to you ... you were destined for the greatness you've been dreaming about. God gave you the vision and he will make provisions if you just believe! Jesus really does mean for us to move mountains. He wants us to live in the bold joy of knowing that nothing will be impossible for us. I'll see you at the top!

Day 18
Likeability & Diligence

People hire people because they like them; they keep them because they're good.

SCRIPTURE

A sluggard's appetite is never filled, but the desires of the diligent are fully satisfied.

PROVERBS 13:4 (NIV)

The principle of focus for the day is likeability and diligence. I always say, and I truly believe in this, that people hire you because they like you. However, they keep you because you're good. I will never forget when I was a tour publicist for Chris Brown. His manager at the time, Tina Davis, was having a conversation with someone and I happened to overhear. I heard them asking her about my background and lack of experience in the music industry, yet Tina had hired me and given me an executive level position. Her answer was simple. She had a good feeling about me and that if I messed up, it was on me because she was giving me the opportunity of a life time.

I was just 25 at the time, but in that moment, I realized that people hire you because they like you, but they keep you because you're good. So, I called on my mentors, I sought counsel; I made sure I was extra equipped. I knew operating in the spirit of excellence would make me stand out. I knew that being diligent would be greatly rewarded, and I was brought on again in 2007/2008.

PRAYER

Dear God, guide me to where my uniqueness is rewarded. Show me that which you want me to be diligent over. Prepare me for the opportunities you have in my future. I thank you in advance for all victories in Jesus' name, amen.

DECLARATIONS

To be recited out loud in front of the mirror with your right hand on your heart.

I AM EXCELLENT.

MY DILIGENCE IS REWARDED.

MY UNIQUENESS IS ACKNOWLEDGED.

I AM A SOLUTION TO SOMEONE'S PROBLEM.

I AM GRATEFUL FOR EVERY MOMENT TO DEMONSTRATE GOD'S GREATNESS.

EXERCISE

Identify an open door in your life and business and write it down. Now write down three things that you can do to better excel at that opportunity. Really stretch yourself to ultimate greatness.

FEARLESS FEMALE ENTREPRENEUR SPOTLIGHT

Alex Evjen

Stylist & Blogger

I was a gangly, awkward girl who always went unnoticed. I was average at everything in the top half of my class and never won an award for any achievement. I wore cardigans and flip-flops exclusively, and I meandered through life just existing. But on the inside I was a girl who dreamed big dreams of being someone that mattered, someone that made a difference, someone that people remembered.

When God placed a passion for fashion design on my heart I finally felt like I was motivated to achieve something big. At the same time, I knew I didn't look like any of the girls that worked in the fashion world. However, I kept my sights on fashion and I trusted God to move from Texas to Arizona to obtain a marketing degree. Only I didn't make it into the business school and doubt filled my heart. Defeated, I fell back to meandering through life ignoring my love for fashion and style. I kept wearing my cardigans and soon found myself at a desk job in PR. Four years after getting my first job, I was depressed and feeling as if life was passing me by. I was purposeless and passionless. Longing for heaven or a substantial change, God reminded me that fashion was something I still loved.

Feeling like I was at rock bottom, I decided to start my own styling company with no fashion education to my name and nothing to lose. AVE Styles was born and I began chipping away at the mountain of fashion believing that God would make a way but still thinking it was impossible. Until one day when this new social media tool called Pinterest fell into my lap. I started to use it for my styling clients, and I became obsessed. It was almost overnight that I grew to having over a million followers on this new tool. I had no idea what this would mean or what to do with this new-found popularity, but soon Glamour Magazine was knocking on my door and I was being flown to L.A. and New York City to host parties.

The president of Neiman Marcus called me to ask for advice on how to sell clothes online and Anthropologie asked me to style decor for them. I had made it into the fashion industry in the blink of an eye and in the most unforeseen way. It had God written all over it. God made the impossible possible.

Along the way, I became what the social media world calls an "influencer." An influencer is someone who can positively or negatively influence people through social media. I have chosen to use my influence for good and to remind the unseen women that they matter and are heard. Fashion is still a love of mine, but more than that God has revealed my true passion is bringing hope to those who don't have it.

Day 19
Your Network & Your Circle

*Being in the right circle is about being around the
right energy.*

SCRIPTURE

As iron sharpens iron, so one person sharpens another.

PROVERBS 27:17 (NIV)

We've all heard the saying, "Your network, equals your net worth." When you actually witness this take place in your life, then you know it's real. When I first started my PR Company, a service based business in the entertainment industry, I had to make every move count. There was no room for me to spend any time at events that didn't pertain to my industry because it wouldn't have made business sense. I had to be in places where potential clients would be. When people truly understand this principle, they start spending their time in ways that can be monetized. They surround themselves with potential clients or resources that can lead to prosperous business opportunities.

If you're trying to get a million dollar investment and you're hanging around people who only make six figures, who can make sure you meet that goal? Even if you are not trying to get an investment that large, you need to position yourself to make sure you reach the target audience in need of your products and services. You want to make sure you are properly positioned for success.

I utilized my network from college to help jumpstart my career. When Coach Carter opened the door and showed me that movie studios outsource for PR and Marketing work, I immediately called Will Packer and Rob Hardy, FAMU grads who owned a production company. I was able to service many of their film projects, which lead to more opportunities to work on other large films.

I also tell people, "Change your circle and you'll change your life." This principle can be applied to your well-being as a whole. You need to make sure that you have cheerleaders in your corner, as well as people with wisdom. Being in the right circle is about being around the right energy. Energy is transferred, just like you learned in sciences. It's never destroyed. It's transferred from one matter to another, from one source to another. You need to be around the right energy in order to produce the right results.

If you desire different results, you may need to change your circle. That doesn't mean go deleting people out your phone or off your social media sites. You may need to compartmentalize your life and place them in the appropriate categories. Everybody doesn't belong in your bedroom. Everybody doesn't belong at your kitchen table. Everybody doesn't belong in your living room. If you're looking for different results, you need to connect with different people. Life is about growth.

PRAYER

Dear Heavenly Father, show me where the ground is fertile. Show me where you want me to sow my time and resources to produce the maximum harvest. Lord, I trust your guidance in leading me in the right direction for the right results. In Jesus' name, Amen.

DECLARATIONS

To be recited out loud in front of the mirror with your right hand on your heart.

I SEEK GREAT COUNSEL.

I HAVE CHEERLEADERS IN MY CORNER.

I AM PROPERLY POSITIONED FOR SUCCESS.

I SURROUND MYSELF WITH POSITIVE ENERGY.

I SPEND MY TIME AND ENERGY IN AREAS THAT ARE FRUITFUL.

EXERCISE

What are three events pertaining to your business and industry that you should attend? Begin preparing and making plans to attend. My suggestion is select one with potential clients, one for continued education, and one for personal growth and self-care. You may have potential clients at all three but this is a guide to make sure you have these areas covered as a female entrepreneur.

FEARLESS FEMALE ENTREPRENEUR SPOTLIGHT

Bricia and Paulina Lopez

Co-Owners of Guelaguetza

We grew up in a catholic household and remember visiting church with our grandma on Sundays back when we lived in Mexico. Though we remember her faith and devotion, the spirit of the church never really captured us. Our parents weren't devoted church goers either, it was a place we visited only a few times a year. When we moved to Los Angeles, those few times a year because fewer and fewer. Both of us have worked in our family business all of our lives and in 2007 when the recession hit the country, it affected every part of our lives. Our parents were in the brink of a divorce and bankruptcy. Our mom was invited to a Christian church by a friend who saw how her family was coming apart. When her and my dad were working their marriage out, my mom agreed to give him a final chance, under one condition - that he go with her to church. Our dad went with her week after week and both accepted Jesus into their life together. The day that happened, God began to manifest himself into our lives. It was a real miracle to see our parents back together and how he was changing who they were as people. Both of us began attending church with them every Sunday at that time. We resisted at first, but our pastor was a true blessing into our lives.

Our faith Journey is ongoing, but it is what definitely keeps us centered and what we attribute our success to. One of our most favorite bible verses is "For I know the plans I have for you, declares the Lord." At times where we think our world is falling apart, we always go back to this verse. It brings us peace and keeps us facing forward. To think where we used to be, and acknowledging where we are today, makes us realize and aware how much he has blessed us over and over again and that we are truly part of a bigger plan. Today we attend Oasis in Los Angeles. We continue to see miracles in our lives and are now seeing how our faith can impact our own families. We are both mothers and there's no greater gift to give our children, then the gift of a relationship with God. Every morning ask for patience, resilience and wisdom. Believe us, he is listening.

Day 20
Protect Your Gift

Give your gift to people who treasure it.

SCRIPTURE

Do not give dogs what is sacred; do not throw your pearls to pigs.

MATTHEW 7:6 (NIV)

Today's tip is on protecting your gift. The Bible says that our gifts make room for us and brings us before great men. Protect your gift because if you abuse it, give it away frivolously, or do anything reckless with it, then it can't bring you before great men. For example, I work and I've had the privilege to work with the very high-end clientele. I have to protect those relationships, as well as the gift inside of me that attracted those relationships. Please don't get this message confused, I never mean be selfish. This message is not for the overguarded individual who needs to loosen his/her reins. This is for those that overgive in abundance all the time, like me; you have to be conscious of the recipients of their gifts.

In our Fearless Business Club, the ladies can always attest that I am willing to share my resources. If I have a resource that can help them in their industry, I give it freely. I always want to make sure everyone is leveling up. I like to see everybody win. This is my nature. But in general, we also have to remember to protect our gifts. There are people who don't see the value in everyone's hard work. It is good to be a cheerful and generous giver, but you need to give your gift to people who treasure it. Give to people who recognize your gift and value it. Anybody who treats you as less than you're worth is abusing you and should not have access to you.

PRAYER

Dear God, you know I am a cheerful giver with a generous heart. Show me how to place my gifts in the hands of people who value me and what you have placed inside of me. Lead me in the way everlasting, in Jesus' name, amen.

DECLARATIONS

To be recited out loud in front of the mirror with your right hand on your heart.

PEOPLE IN MY CIRCLE CHERISH ME.

I SEE WHAT I HAVE TO OFFER AS VALUABLE.

I OFFER MY GIFTS WHERE THEY ARE VALUED.

I SURROUND MYSELF WITH THOSE WHO SEE MY VALUE.

I DELIGHT WHEN OTHERS ARE GREAT STEWARDS OVER THE GIFT I GIVE THEM.

EXERCISE

Meditation is your exercise for today. Sit cross-legged on the floor with your palms up and relaxed on your knees. Breathe in and out gently while remaining conscious of your breathing. See yourself being a generous giver, and envision those to whom you are giving as being excellent stewards over what they have been given. Delight in their fruitfulness.

FEARLESS FEMALE ENTREPRENEUR SPOTLIGHT

Sharlinda Parker & Sabrina Rowe

Owners of TuLa2 Nail Salon & Company

It's often said that two heads are better than one, and Sabrina Rowe and Sharlinda Rowe-Parker, owners of Tu La 2 Salon & Company, are proof positive. We've never been procrastinators, so as Richmond, Virginia-born twin sisters we set our entrepreneurial sites on the beauty industry immediately after high school and the grace of God has covered us ever since. The idea was to use our hands to touch the hands of others and offer services that were anchored in love, friendship and faith.

Upon receiving our nail tech certification, we sprang into action and began building our business. After years of professional success in and around the Virginia area, we intuitively decided to move to the bustling city of Atlanta, Georgia, where we knew our empire, influence and aesthetic, could grow beyond our wildest dreams. Once in Atlanta, we knew something needed to separate us from our contemporaries and place us ahead of the pack. So "luxury" became our governing platform and we secured employment at a high-end salon in the upscale area of Buckhead.

While there, we noticed another gap in the industry when upper-level executives and celebrities didn't want to make routine visits to the salon. In response, we began to offer private treatments through mobile services at our clients' homes and offices.

We landed many of the city's music industry elite as our clients and our professionalism and quality of services began to spread rapidly. All the while, we still made a commitment to continue our education in the field and garnered multiple certifications in booming techniques.

In January 2002, we took a leap of faith and formed Tu La 2 Nail Salon & Company, which celebrated our 15-year anniversary in 2017 with the opening of a luxe new salon in Atlanta's highly-popular West Midtown neighborhood. Since our introduction, as entrepreneurs we have amassed a clientele list that reads like a Hollywood who's who dossier—coveted names include Beyoncé, Queen Latifah, Ben Stiller, Dallas Austin, Demi Moore, Katherine Heigl, Tyler Perry, Faith Evans, Usher and Martin Lawrence.

Our signature services (which include a coveted hand-buffing technique and special services designed for customers with health issues like diabetes) have been instrumental in helping us eclipse the industry. Lifestyle, Paramount and brands from Pepsi to Lionsgate Films to FOX pictures to Neiman Marcus have all tapped on us to enhance groundbreaking commercials and photo campaigns with their impeccable nail work.

Upping the ante, Tu La 2 imprint was featured in the historic final season of programming on the Style Network in the Buckhead based television series, Big Rich Atlanta. Viewers were privy to our style, flair and sparkly aesthetic weekly, in and out of the salon. In demand for both service and savvy, we have also been profiled on the pages of Upscale, UPTOWN, The Atlantan, Jezebel, Ebony and ESSENCE magazines. Additionally, as of February 2017, Sisters United ATL, an organization formed by Parker with Rowe's guidance to support the spiritual and emotional well-being of women, has taken up monthly residency in the new salon. Parker states,

"If you serve God and his people, he'll do the rest."

Rowe continues, "It's unbelievable that in all of our years of business, we've never done marketing or any big push. We've grown as a result of us giving love to our customers and them giving it back."

Day 21
Purpose Over Popularity

You are here to serve the people that God assigned to you.

SCRIPTURE

Just as the Son of Man did not come to be served, but to serve, and to give his life as a ransom for many.

MATTHEW 20:28 (NIV)

Today's principle is on purpose over popularity. In this digital age, people just want to be popular and become famous for no good reason at all. What happened to wanting to be great and wanting to make an impact in whatever you gifts are? Purpose over popularity.

We actually talk about this often in my Fearless Discussions, specifically the discussion entitled "Is It All for the Fame?" There was once a time where making a positive impact on others' lives is what was rewarded in society. We must get back to the place where we're acknowledging people for their greatness and for the impact that helped to change the world. People weren't famous for taking pictures and having thousands of followers on social media.

I had an intern once tell me that she didn't see the benefit in being classy. She went on to list examples, such as the women on the television show Basketball Wives. She said these women reaped great benefits without putting in the work, as compared to someone like me who is just as attractive as the women on the show but has to work to maintain a successful business. In no way am I throwing shade at the women on that show, but this was an honest perspective of my intern. She wanted to have it easy and she "thought" they did. My intern also knew what I was about and what I stood for. She had no clue if these women were making a positive impact on society and the people around them. I told her that she needed to aim higher in life and that she had a purpose which was greater than her idea of having it easy. I told her that she needed to think about the positive impact she was meant to leave on the people in her circle.

Popularity doesn't guarantee you a fulfilled life but purpose does. Are you doing what you were purposed to do? Statistics say that over 80 percent of people are not happy at their jobs. How could that number be so overwhelming? You are taught to graduate high school, go to college and pick a career. How could the end result be such a high percentage of unhappy people? Something is wrong with this statistic which begs the question as to whether people do what they are programmed to do versus purposed to do.

I believe in higher education, as I am a graduate of Florida A & M University, and I have a bachelor's and master's degree. But what if you were supposed to just learn a trade? Did you have to go this so called "popular" route to get there and now you aren't even happy?

There is still time for you to live on purpose because the world is such a greater place when you do. When you live on purpose, you don't compromise your integrity. You make decisions in alignment with your purpose. One of the many things I love about Jesus is that He always stayed on task. There were many times when He was tempted but He made decisions in alignment with His purpose. The most authentic person is always the most attractive, always. And you will always draw great people to you. You will always be attractive when you walk in your purpose.

Don't get caught up in popular social media trends and doing what you see online. Stay in your lane. You are here to serve the people that God assigned to you. In your business, you will have to make choices, but always remember to choose purpose over popularity because what is purposed for you will be popular.

PRAYER

Dear God, I am grateful for the territory, dominion and authority over which you have given me charge. I choose to focus on displaying your character with the guidance of the Holy Spirit. I enjoy and delight in taking shepherd of my flock. In Jesus' name, amen.

DECLARATION

To be recited out loud in front of the mirror with your right hand on your heart.

I HAVE A PURPOSE.

I LIVE ON PURPOSE.

I SERVE ON PURPOSE.

MY PURPOSE IS GREATER THAN I IMAGINED.

I MAKE DECISIONS IN ALIGNMENT WITH MY PURPOSE.

EXERCISE

Do a one-day fast from social media. Journal what your business would look like if social media didn't exist. Social media is not bad; it's a stellar tool. However, this exercise will teach you to take a moment to pause and not get caught up in the rat race. Develop three strategies of growth that are not social media related. Think outside of the box and get creative.

FEARLESS FEMALE ENTREPRENEUR SPOTLIGHT

Marilyn Jones

Founder and Owner of B Fragranced LLC created the Brand [ME]™

B Fragranced is a fragrance and beauty company based out of Chicago. We are a beauty company that caters to both men and women offering the best perfume and colognes along with our hand & body lotions. I'm proud to be minority owned and WBE certified owning 100% of my company.

I'm a Chicago native and number eleven of twelve children born to a devoted mother and father. Unfortunately, at the young age of 5 tragedy struck my family and my mom lost her battle to Breast Cancer. Growing up I had no memories of my mom besides her smell. This birthed a passion and a zeal to create fragrances as unique as the individual who wears it! I always had a love for perfumes and lotions that grew stronger in later years. "Our flagship Fragrance Embellish doesn't smell like my mother once did, but, the blueprint of the business certainly embodies her".

I wanted to create a Brand that aids in you "Celebrating Who You Are", with that said, I branded the creative process of making what "you" wear the pinnacle of a two-letterword characterized as ME. Often times, we as women can be quite territorial when it comes to sharing what we're wearing or there's a certain stigma of "having it all" or "you've arrived" when you share with others that you're wearing a Gucci or Tom Ford fragrance. I've always thought that we're really giving the power to them, so saying that you're wearing [ME] aids in Empowering who you are! Brand who you are, be courageous, be Beautiful more importantly B Fragranced. Leave your memory mark!!

I would not be where I am today without my faith in God! Prior to starting my business, I worked in corporate as a brand finance manager making over a six-figure income. Did I have fears and doubt of walking away frommy corporate life to pursue my dreams? Absolutely, But I also had the Faith in God that he would give me the desires of my heart.

As a woman of faith, I set a non-negotiable, I must stay committed to making time for daily prayer and attending church services. If I'm out traveling, I make sure to stream the service live. This gives me the fuel that I need to make it from week to week.

I also listen to different YouTube sermons from other powerful women such as, Sarah Jakes Roberts & Priscilla Shirer, to help motivate and inspire me because iron sharpens iron. I love to listen to praise and worship music as it gives me hope when I feel hopeless and it gives me power when I feel defeated in my entrepreneur journey. Last but definitely not least, I'm very careful of the company that I keep. I surround myself amongst like-minded people, not just those like-minded friends in terms of business but like-minded in faith too.

Congratulations on completing
FEARLESS Faith + Hustle: *A 21-Day Devotional for the **Fun,
Fly, Fabulous** Female Entrepreneur. I encourage you to keep God
as the head of your life, family, and business!*

ABOUT THE AUTHOR

Arian Simone is an entrepreneur, celebrity publicist, motivational speaker, and author that has been featured in Cosmopolitan, Essence, Huffington Post, Ebony and more. Upon graduating college, Arian Simone was laid off from her job and went from living in her apartment to out of her car. She was without a home of her own for almost a year before she was sought out to do public relations and marketing independently. Building a successful PR and Marketing Firm from the ground up, she established great relationships in the entertainment industry with clients such as the Sony Pictures, Universal Pictures, Walt Disney Pictures and more. She is credited with doing publicity and promotions work on films such as Ride Along, Limitless, Hancock, Takers, and 007: Quantum of Solace just to name a few. She has also serviced clients in the music industry. Her first book My Fabulous & Fearless Journey chronicles the journey from college to the successful professional she is today. She shares her Homeless to Hollywood story with transparency, humor, and vulnerability all around the world!

Other Resourses

Scriptures Found In This Book

Jesus said, "No procrastination. No backward looks. You can't put God's kingdom off till tomorrow. Seize the day."

LUKE 9:62 (MSG)

Where there is no vision, the people perish...

PROVERBS 29:18 (KJV)

Therefore I tell you, do not worry about your life, what you will eat or drink; or about your body, what you will wear. Is not life more than food, and the body more than clothes?

MATTHEW 6:25 (NIV)

...Calls those things which do not exist as though they did.

ROMANS 4:17 (NKJV)

Finally, brothers and sisters, whatever is true, whatever is noble, whatever is right, whatever is pure, whatever is lovely, whatever is admirable—if anything is excellent or praiseworthy—think about such things.

PHILIPPIANS 4:8 (NIV)

What, then, shall we say in response to these things? If God is for us, who can be against us?

ROMANS 8:31 (NIV)

A man's gift maketh room for him, and bringeth him before great men.

PROVERBS 18:16 (KJV)

A man's gift maketh room for him, and bringeth him before great men.

PROVERBS 18:16 (KJV)

Many are the plans in a person's heart, but it is the Lord's purpose that prevails.

PROVERBS 19:21 (NIV)

Now to Him who is able to do exceedingly abundantly above all that we ask or think, according to the power that works in us, to Him be glory in the church by Christ Jesus to all generations, forever and ever. Amen.

EPHESIANS 3:20-21 (NJKV)

Well done, good and faithful servant! You have been faithful with a few things; I will put you in charge of many things. Come and share your master's happiness!

MATTHEW 25:23 (NIV)

She did what she could.

MARK 14:8 (NIV)

Now thanks be unto God, which always causeth us to triumph in Christ, and maketh manifest the savour of his knowledge by us in every place.

2 CORINTHIANS 2:14 (KJV)

"Martha, Martha," the Lord answered, "You are worried and upset about many things, but few things are needed—or indeed only one. Mary has chosen what is better, and it will not be taken away from her."

LUKE 10: 41–42 (NIV)

"...For I know the plans I have for you," declares the Lord, "plans to prosper you and not to harm you, plans to give you hope and a future."

JEREMIAH 29:11 (NIV)

But let patience have its perfect work, that you may be perfect and complete, lacking nothing.

JAMES 1:4 (NKJV)

But my God shall supply all your needs according to his riches in glory by Christ Jesus.

PHILIPPIANS 4:19 (KJV)

Both you and these people who are with you will surely wear yourselves out. For this thing is too much for you; you are not able to perform it by yourself. Listen now to my voice; I will give you counsel, and God will be with you.

EXODUS 18:18-19 (NKJV)

A sluggard's appetite is never filled, but the desires of the diligent are fully satisfied.

PROVERBS 13:4 (NIV)

As iron sharpens iron, so one person sharpens another.

PROVERBS 27:17 (NIV)

Do not give dogs what is sacred; do not throw your pearls to pigs.

MATTHEW 7:6 (NIV)

Just as the Son of Man did not come to be served, but to serve, and to give his life as a ransom for many.

MATTHEW 20:28 (NIV)

21-Day Fearless Challenge To Being a Better Woman

The 21 Day Fearless Challenge is The Ultimate Lifestyle Challenge and it's FREE! We want you at the highest and best expression of yourself: mind, body, and soul, doing everything in the spirit of excellence. It takes 21 Days to create a habit, and our 21 Day Fearless Challenge is designed to put you in the habit of fun, fly, fabulous living, while being FEARLESS inside and out! The fulfilled life is the best life and you deserve it!

DAY 1 - Burn a Candle and Meditate for 30 min

DAY 2 - Walk for 45 minutes today

DAY 3 - Bless someone or a charity financially {it can be as small as $1 or as large as you choose}

DAY 4 - Read one chapter in a book

DAY 5 - Compliment 5 people today & smile at everyone you encounter

DAY 6 - Listen to a sermon on Womanhood or being an excellent wife

DAY 7 - Find a a new recipe and create the dish

DAY 8 - Journal all that you are grateful

DAY 9 - Recite your favorite scripture at the top of every hour

DAY 10 - Do an in shower breast exam

DAY 11 - Do something new with your hair {get out of you regular routine}

DAY 12 - Visit a fabric store and learn various fabric swatches {purchase a small sewing kit to have on hand}

DAY 13 - Try a new perfume

DAY 14 - Surprise your husband or significant other with a handwritten note of all the things you are thankful that they contribute to your life

DAY 15 - Purchase a piece of shape wear. Also, if it's in budget get a pretty bra and panty set! Feel sexy for you!

DAY 16 - Attend a Yoga Class or do in home Yoga from a YouTube link

DAY 17 - Exfoliate your skin: treat your skin to a body scrub

DAY 18 - Treat someone to Lunch today

DAY 19 - Share words of wisdom with a young girl

DAY 20 - Decorate or organize something minor in your home

DAY 21 - Go to the MAC counter and get your makeup done or
get a professional make up artist to do your face

365
FEARLESS QUOTES

1. Never let your fear decide your fate
2. The happiest people make the most of everything
3. There is no greater discovery than self-discovery
4. You will never learn if you don't make mistakes, you will never be successful if you don't try
5. The more you praise and celebrate your life, the more there is in life to celebrate
6. Turn your passion into profit
7. Today's struggle is helping you develop the strength you need for tomorrow
8. Faith can move mountains, start pushing
9. Any age is the perfect age to follow your dreams
10. Be the kind of woman who, when your feet hit the floor in the morning the devil says, oh no she's up
11. Wear your passion and dress for success
12. Don't worry if you mess up you can still learn from it
13. Try it one more time
14. Do one thing every day that scares you
15. Faith is seeing light in every situations
16. Faith is seeing light in every situations
17. Faith makes things possible
18. If you believe, you will receive whatever you ask for in prayer Matthew 21:22
19. Never let the fear of striking out keep you from playing the game
20. Excellence can be achieved if you . . . risk more than others think is safe, love more than others think is wise, dream more than others think is practical, and expect more than others think is possible
21. We come to love not by finding a perfect person, but by learning to see an imperfect person perfectly
22. Your attitude is your altitude. It determines how high you fly
23. The difference between try and triumph is a little umph
24. Excellence is never an accident; it is the result of high intention, sincere effort, intelligent direction, skillful execution and the vision to see obstacles as opportunities
25. If you want your dreams to come true, you must wake them up
26. Blessed are those who can give without remembering and take

without forgetting

27. What's the point of being alive if you don't at least try to do something remarkable?
28. Worry looks around, fear looks back, faith looks up
29. Being happy doesn't mean that everything is perfect. It means that you've decided to look beyond the imperfections
30. A battle worth fighting is between who you are and who you want to be
31. Sometimes we are limited more by attitude than by opportunities
32. A winner never quits and a quitter never wins
33. Great results require great ambitions
34. It is the size of one's will, which determines success
35. It only takes a single thought to move the world
36. Take no challenge lightly - strive for excellence
37. The key to happiness is freedom, and the key to freedom is courage
38. Until you spread your wings, you'll have no idea if you can fly
39. Remember that great love and great achievements involve great risk
40. Courage is not the absence of fear, it is the conquest of it
41. For I am the Lord, your God, who takes hold of your right hand and says to you, Do not fear; I will help you. (Isaiah 41:13)
42. Be strong and courageous. Do not be afraid or terrified because of them, for the Lord your God goes with you; he will never leave you nor forsake you. (Deuteronomy 31:6)
43. Faith is like electricity. You can't see it, but you can see the light
44. Encouragement is the oxygen of the soul
45. Some people dream of great accomplishments, while others stay awake and do them
46. Hope sees the invisible, feels the intangible and achieves the impossible
47. Hope is putting faith to work when doubting would be easier
48. Successful leaders have the courage to take action where others hesitate
49. Character is a victory, not a gift
50. "In seeking happiness for others, you find it for yourself
51. Learn from yesterday, live for today, hope for tomorrow
52. There are no short cuts going anywhere worth going

53. It is better to live your own destiny imperfectly than to live an imitation of somebody else's life with perfection
54. Walk in faith, not by sight 2 Corinthians 5:7
55. "To have faith is to be sure of the things we hope for, to be certain of the things we cannot see." Hebrews 11:1
56. It is never too late to be what you might have been
57. Dream what you want to dream, go where you want to do
58. You only have one life and one chance to do all the things you want to do
59. Good things come to people who wait, but better things come to those who go out and get them
60. Do not be fooled. Success is not the key to happiness. Happiness is the key to success
61. You don't have to wait for the storm to pass. Go be awesome in the rain.
62. The time is now. Start living the life you imagined
63. I refuse to believe the sky is the limit when there are footprints on the moon
64. Goals are the bridge between your past and your potential
65. Today is the perfect day to start living your dreams
66. Everyday is a new beginning
67. Be the best version of you
68. People who are pursuing their dreams should not be interrupted by those aren't
69. Never give up on something that you can't go a day without thinking about
70. Never stop doing your best just because someone doesn't give you credit
71. Don't be afraid, just believe Mark 5:36
72. People hire you because they like you, they just keep you because you are good
73. Enjoy every moment and God will give you more moments to enjoy!
74. If you feel your dream is too big, its because you need God's help with it
75. What we think, we become
76. Never give up on your dream just because of the time it will take to

accomplish them. Time will pass anyway

77. Nothing is ever falling apart its always falling into place
78. Don't eat with anyone that is going to brag about feeding you
79. People these days gain attention by losing respect, maintain your dignity, your time will come
80. Where there is love and inspiration, you can't go wrong
81. Take risks: If you win you will be happy, if you lose you will be wise
82. Faith tells me that no matter what lies ahead of me, God is already there
83. Life is like a camera; Focus on what's important, capture the good times, develop from the negatives and if it goes wrong...Take another shot
84. Create the life you can't wait to wake up to
85. Think about how far you've come today and how much further you'll go tomorrow
86. Keep your head, heels and standards high
87. It takes great courage to change your life. The truth is you can do anything, but you've got to believe it
88. You have to love yourself before anyone else can take the role of loving you
89. God will always give you the pieces to the puzzle; it's just up to you to put them together
90. Some times you have to switch gears to get to the next level
91. Anyone trying to bring you down is already below you
92. Don't ever let average distract you from amazing
93. Even if you stumble, you're still moving forward
94. You are altogether beautiful, my love' there is no flaw in you. Song of Solomon 4:7
95. Some pursue happiness, others create it
96. Let your faith guide you to your destiny
97. One day your life will flash before your eyes. Make sure it's worth watching
98. I am fearfully and wonderfully made. Psalm 139:3
99. Happiness is a choice
100. To create more positive results in your life, replace 'if only' with 'next time.'

101. Live today to the fullest
102. Get up and Go GET IT
103. Life is not a dress rehearsal. Enjoy it now
104. Organize your life around your dreams - and watch them come true
105. The most attractive person is the most authentic person
106. God is always opening many doors, you just need to walk through them
107. When you do his work he sends his people
108. Giving is the Best Gift you could ever receive
109. If you are getting a "no" you are asking the wrong question or talking to the wrong person
110. Never tell your problems to someone who can't provide a solution
111. Your Network = Your Net Worth
112. You have to seize the moment, many opportunities can come your way, but a moment can never be relived
113. Live Fearlessly
114. Great people bring out the great in people
115. You attract what you are
116. Anyone who dares to waste an hour of your time has not discovered its value
117. Dress how you want to be addressed
118. For where I am headed there is no turning back
119. If a negative thought comes across your mind, replace it with a positive thought
120. Make your vision so clear that your fears become irrelevant
121. It's meaningless to work in a job you are not passionate about
122. Wake up. It's time to turn those dreams into reality
123. Live your life on purpose
124. If your dream job doesn't exist, create it
125. Face Everything And Rise (F.E.A.R)
126. May your faith always exceed your fears
127. I cheated on my FEARS, broke up with my DOUBTS, got engaged with FAITH, and now I'm marrying my Dreams
128. A fearless life = a limitless life
129. Live fearlessly and watch the world change before your eyes
130. A new day is a new chance to have new beginnings

131. Free yourself from the chains of fear
132. You will never know how amazing you will be unless you try
133. Trust your intuition
134. Don't be pushed by your problems, be lead by your dreams
135. No beauty shines greater than that of a good heart
136. Beauty attracts the eye but personality captures the heart
137. Life is your canvas, paint it beautifully
138. If you don't jump you will never know if you could fly
139. All the greats did not let fear get in the way
140. Don't be afraid to get back up, to try again, to love again, to live again and to dream again
141. Listen to the voice within telling you to do it
142. She turned her cants into cans and her dreams into plans
143. The lord himself will fight for you, just stay calm Exodus 14:14
144. Don't let anyone ever dull your sparkle
145. You cannot change what you tolerate
146. The phrase 'do not be afraid' is written in the Bible 365 times. That's a daily reminder from God to live everyday being fearless
147. What's your dream?
148. I have no time for conditional friends
149. You can't run from your gifts
150. You have to be disciplined follower to be a disciplined leader
151. My response to everything in life is....I TRUST GOD
152. Favor can bring you things that money can't buy
153. Don't make permanent decisions on temporary situations or don't make long term decisions with short term matters
154. You are destined for greatness
155. Something wonderful is about to happen
156. Your are one idea away from your next breakthrough
157. Put God First and you will never be last
158. Sometimes you have to create what you want to be a part of
159. Most of all let love guide your life - Col 3:14
160. You know the truth by the way it feels
161. The first step to getting what you want is having the courage to get rid of what you don't
162. Don't worry. God is always on time. Trust Him

163. Queens Inspire Kings
164. Don't Give up what you want most for what you want now
165. Little girls with big dreams become women with vision
166. Those who patiently preserve will truly receive a reward without measure
167. Wake up with determination and go to bed with satisfaction
168. Don't lose a diamond while chasing glitter
169. I refuse to be anything less than successful
170. I will fight for you, you need only to be still. - Exodus 14:14
171. The moment you're ready to quit is usually the moment right before a miracle happens. Don't give up
172. What I'm after cannot be purchased
173. Invest in yourself you can afford it, trust me
174. One small positive thought in the morning can change your whole day
175. Believe it will happen
176. Stop being afraid of what could go wrong and think of what could go right
177. When overcoming obstacles and pursuing your dreams you have to be FEARLESS
178. I can only show you something real, I can't make you appreciate it.
179. Remember why you started
180. God got me
181. I write my own story
182. Everything that glitters isn't gold
183. A flower does not think of competing to the flower next to it, it just blooms
184. Be Intentional
185. Use your time, talent and money to make a positive impact on the world
186. A roadblock doesn't mean stop. There is always an alternative route. Keep Going!
187. If you aren't going all the way, why go at all?
188. Fear is a Liar
189. Be Legendary
190. Be Great On Purpose

191. God is faithful yesterday, today and tomorrow
192. Stop pressing the snooze button of life, get up and make things happen
193. Do the right thing even when no one is looking
194. How someone handles Power is a true testament of their character
195. Good Morning. I'll be handing all your problems today, so relax and enjoy the day. Love God
196. You need a dream team
197. If you are persistent you will get it, if you are consistent you will keep it
198. Go where you are celebrated not tolerated
199. Team works makes the dream work
200. Fear is nothing more than an obstacle in the way of success
201. The secret to getting ahead is getting started
202. Work hard in silence let success be your noise
203. Some people dream about success others wake up and work hard for it
204. The dream is free the hustle is sold separately
205. Be an example to others of all that is good in this world, for others will copy you & they also will become good examples
206. Our thanks to God should always precede our requests
207. Be brave enough to dream, and strong enough to act
208. Everyday is a gift, that's why they call it the present
209. If you want to achieve greatness stop asking for permission
210. "If you do not believe in yourself, very few other people will
211. Those who strive for merit shall attain success
212. Attitude is everything
213. Happiness is not about being perfect but about seeing beyond the imperfections
214. No man can block what God has destined for you
215. Miracles are on the way, keep the faith
216. If you're still looking for the one person to change your life, take a look in the mirror
217. Just when the caterpillar thought the world was over, it became a butterfly
218. Faith achieves the impossible

219. Be patient, live life, have faith
220. True beauty is not outer appearance; it's located in the heart and soul, reflected in one's eyes
221. Blessed and Highly favored - Luke 1:28
222. "Where there's a will, there's a way
223. To be good is not enough when you dream of being great.
224. To the brave and the faithful, nothing is impossible
225. The bigger the challenge, the greater the opportunity
226. Live by your word, lead by example
227. Success doesn't come from waiting for great things; it comes from making them happen
228. Dare to succeed
229. Reality starts in the mind. Actions must take place to make thoughts real
230. Either make your money work for you, or you will always work for your money
231. When you are confident in your ability to achieve what you want in life, you will also be free of fear
232. The first step to succeeding is believing that you can succeed
233. All the rewards life has to offer can be yours, you just have to try
234. Success takes work and faith
235. Only dreams believed become dreams achieved
236. Now faith is assurance of things hoped for, a conviction of things not seen."(Hebrews 11:1)
237. Trust in His timing, rely on His promises, wait for His answers, believe in His miracles, rejoice in His goodness, relax in His presence
238. Love without limits Matthew 5:38
239. Never let go of your dreams
240. Don't lose hope, when the sun goes down the stars come out
241. The world doesn't reward perfectionists. It rewards those who get things done
242. Wisdom is knowing what to do next, skill is knowing how to do it virtue is doing it
243. If God is the DJ, then life is the dance floor, love is the rhythm and you are the music

244. Worrying will never change the outcome
245. Replace fear of the unknown with curiosity
246. You are confined only by the walls you build yourself
247. "Together we can change the world, one good deed at a time
248. My dreams are not to big, your mind is just too small
249. Your flaws are perfect for the heart that is meant to love you
250. The only person you should try to be better than is the person you were yesterday
251. A bird sitting on a tree is never afraid of the branch breaking. Because her trust is not in the branch but in her own wings
252. When the world says, 'Give up,' hope whispers, "Try it one more time."
253. Friends are quiet angels who sit on our shoulders and lift our wings when we forget how to fly
254. Believe in your dreams and they may come true; believe in yourself and they will come true."
255. The is no secret to success, just hard work
256. There will never be a perfect time to pursue your dreams & goals. Do it now
257. "Rule #1 of life. Do what makes YOU happy."
258. Self-confidence is the best outfit. Rock it and own it
259. You attract people by the qualities you display. You keep them by the qualities you possess
260. Don't lower your standards for anyone or anything. Self-respect is everything
261. Stop saying 'I wish' and start saying 'I will'
262. To win, all you need to do is get up one more time than you fall down
263. Carry yourself like a queen and you'll attract a king
264. No man can stop, what God has already started
265. When God says yes, No man can say no
266. Don't raise your voice, improve your argument
267. Don't be afraid of the space between your dreams and reality. If you can dream it, you can make it
268. Success is what happens when 10,000 hours of preparation meet with one moment of opportunity

269. Many fine things can be done in a day if you don't always make that day tomorrow

270. "Accept your past without regret, handle your present with confidence, and face your future without fear."

271. "Your value doesn't decrease based on someone's inability to see your worth."

272. In Life quitting is never an option

273. Chase your dreams

274. Dream until your dream comes true

275. When your love for life is unconditional, you will find true happiness

276. You've got what it takes, but it's going to take all you've got

277. Procrastination is the grave in which opportunity is buried

278. When you stop chasing the wrong things, you give the right things a chance to catch you

279. Never let success go to your head. Never let failure go to your heart

280. Attitudes are contagious. Is yours worth catching?

281. The past is a place of reference, not a place of residence

282. When a fearless heart believes, miracles happen

283. Speak it into existence

284. Great things don't come from comfort zones

285. Take every risk, drop every fear

286. Stay true to yourself

287. Experts were once beginners

288. Master your craft

289. Your destiny is designed by God and can never be changed by a man

290. Dreams create desires; desires create determination, determination leads us to our destiny

291. Devote yourself to an idea, Go make it happen

292. Don't you forget: this is your dream

293. Doubt kills more dreams than failure ever will

294. Create a life that feels good on the inside not one that just looks good on the outside

295. Live life happy

296. Stop wishing start doing

297. Worry less do more
298. Don't let fear of the unknown block you from your blessings
299. Freedom is a choice
300. Life the life you imagined
301. Celebrate the small victories
302. Your victory is your testimony
303. Thoughts become things
304. You deserve the best that life has to offer
305. Change is good, embrace it
306. Happiness starts with you
307. Perfection is an allusion
308. You are beautiful
309. Love starts within
310. You are stronger wiser and better than you were yesterday
311. Get out of your own way
312. Rise up and be the best you can be because the world is waiting for you
313. It's time to live the life you love
314. Unlock your gift to the world
315. Sometimes you just have to close your eyes and jump
316. I'm not just confident, I'm Godfident
317. I'm not here to be average, I am here to be awesome
318. Beautiful minds inspire others
319. Never hope for it more than you work for it
320. I will win
321. By courage I repel adversity
322. "You have achieved success if you have lived well, laughed often and loved much."
323. My strength and confidence comes from within
324. Opportunity always comes disguised as hard work
325. Fear is nothing more than an illusion
326. There can be no progress without change
327. Life is too short to be left building someone else's dream
328. Fight for your dreams
329. It's time to start living a FEARLESS life now
330. Perfect love expels all fear - 1 John 4:18

331. Everything you want is on the other side of fear
332. There is no courage without fear
333. Living on purpose is the greatest gift you have to offer
334. Choose faith over fear
335. Turn your dreams into reality, live the life you imagined
336. Fearlessness is knowing you will fly when others say you'll fall
337. The greatest please is living your purpose
338. Nobody said the road would be easy, they did promise it would be worth it
339. Stop letting fears block your blessing. Get up and go get it!
340. It's time. Go get your Blessing
341. Big things often have small beginnings
342. Say goodbye to fear, say hello to success
343. We have to let go to live the life planned for us
344. In every race there are a few obstacles, but there is no greater feeling than that of the finish line
345. Live to work or work for a living, the choice is yours
346. Don't let what you view as financial stability block you of your destiny
347. I can. I will, I'll conquer
348. Trust the process
349. Love is fearless
350. Dream, Believe, Achieve
351. Be brave, be bold, be fearless
352. It's amazing how everything falls into place once you start living on purpose
353. Fear is a liar
354. When you do His work He sends His people
355. People hire you because they like you, they just keep you because you are good
356. Giving is the best gift you could ever receive
357. The most attractive person is the most authentic person
358. If you are getting a "no" you are asking the wrong question or talking to the wrong person
359. Nothing is ever falling apart its always falling into place
360. Never tell your problems to someone who can't provide a solution

361. Your network = Your net worth
362. You have to seize the moment, many opportunities can come your way, but a moment can never be relieved
363. Live fearlessly
364. If you want insta success you will insta fail
365. Just because something is not your fault doesn't mean it's not your responsibility

CPSIA information can be obtained
at www.ICGtesting.com
Printed in the USA
LVHW050727121218
599926LV00001B/1/P